"Benjamins contributes another volume to the important *Loci communes* series by translating a section that treats one of theology's thorniest conundrums: How do we square God's absolute and active governance of the world with human freedom and personal responsibility? Or, as Sophocles would have put it (to give a nod to the humanism that Vermigli so embraced), can we blame Oedipus for murdering his father and marrying his mother when the gods foreordained it before his birth? Benjamins provides a learned introduction that situates Vermigli's thought on the matter in the context of ancient philosophical and humanistic ideas on providence and fate along with their reception and adaptation in Medieval Scholasticism. In doing so, he details the complex web of influences behind Vermigli's approach to the problem, identifying Aristotle and Augustine as two major sources for his choice of vocabulary and categories of thought. As for the text itself, Benjamins admirably translates with his reader always in view. He manages to avoid the stiff, archaic, Latinized English that could make a text like this impenetrable and instead offers a precise but eminently readable and modern version. Kudos for a job well done!"

—**KIRK SUMMERS**
Director of the Classics Program at the University of Alabama

"Peter Martyr Vermigli is undoubtedly one of the most significant Reformed theologians of the sixteenth century and his *Common Places* is the crown jewel of his collected works. The rendering of this work into contemporary

English is a great service to the understanding of Reformation thought and will be enriching for scholars and pastors alike. Vermigli's theological training and acumen are on full display here and the results are rightly esteemed as a masterwork of Reformed theology."

—JORDAN J. BALLOR
The Acton Institute, Junius Institute, author of Covenant, Causality, and Law: A Study in the Theology of Wolfgang Musculus

"According to Peter Martyr Vermigli, the supreme end and highest good in life is to be justified in Christ, accepted in love by the eternal Father. However, it is impossible to appreciate the significance of this acceptance until one has first grasped the catastrophic problem of original sin, the desolate pit from which God raises sinners to make them saints. In addition to answering critical questions surrounding the doctrine (i.e., What is sin? Who is responsible for it? And how does it spread?), this volume showcases Peter Martyr's convictions on a host of related topics including divine creation, humanity's *infidelitas*, total depravity, sexual relations, *imago Dei*, natural gifts, and the necessity of imputed righteousness as the basis for divine favor."

—CHRIS CASTALDO
Lead Pastor of New Covenant Church, Naperville., author of Justified in Christ: The Doctrines of Peter Martyr Vermigli and John Henry Newman

"In 1563, not long after the death of Peter Martyr Vermigli in Zurich, Theodore Beza urged on Heinrich Bullinger the need for a systematic theology to be compiled from Vermigli's immense corpus of scriptural commentary—"*eine Dogmatik in nuce.*" Owing in good part to Anthony Marten's Elizabethan translation, Vermigli's *Common Places* became one of the most influential of all Reformed systematic theologies, especially in the English-speaking world. Kirk Summers has made a selection of these commonplaces pertaining to the pivotal Christian teaching concerning Original Sin and rendered them into lucid, legible, modern English. For any scholar or aspiring theologian attuned to the Reformed tradition this volume should be obligatory reading."

—W.J. TORRANCE KIRBY
McGill University, author of The Zurich Connection and Tudor Political Theology

"With this precise but grandly readable translation, Reformation scholars owe a debt of gratitude to the editors and translator for this initial volume in this new series on Peter Martyr Vermigli's *Common Places*. Kirk Summers has faithfully and eloquently rendered Vermigli who is here at his subtle and forceful best; and has thus opened to a wider audience the Reformer's thought on some of the questions most central to the disputes of the sixteenth century: sin, human nature, what imputation entails, and even the nature of sacramental grace. Further, Summers's painstaking apparatus (Vermigli often quoted his sources from memory) lays bare Vermigli's vast command of the literature on these questions. Honor due."

—GARY JENKINS
Eastern University; author of Calvin's Tormentors: Understanding the Conflicts that Shaped the Reformer

"Legend has it that Peter Martyr Vermigli descended out of the Italian Alps as the 'ready-made Reformer,' and his *Common Places* certainly confirm both his reputation and why so many esteemed his work. His *Common Places* were posthumously extracted from his biblical commentaries, which means that they are insightfully exegetical and theological. Students of the Reformation would do well to pick up this book and see for themselves the deep currents that run through his work. Students of Scripture will also greatly profit from one who knows the Bible so well."

—J. V. FESKO

Harriet Barbour Professor of Systematic and Historical Theology, Reformed Theological Seminary, Jackson, Mississippi

"Vermigli was one of the most important theologians of the sixteenth century. His *Loci Communes* is a collated summary of his theology and I am delighted to see this part of it made accessible in a new translation to an English speaking readership."

—DR. ROBERT LETHAM

Professor of Systematic & Historical Theology, Union School of Theology, Wales, UK

PETER MARTYR VERMIGLI
COMMON PLACES:

On Providence & the Cause of Sin

PETER MARTYR VERMIGLI COMMON PLACES:
ON PROVIDENCE & THE CAUSE OF SIN

Translated and Edited by Joshua Benjamins

DAVENANT PRESS 2024

Copyright © 2024 The Davenant Institute
All rights reserved.

ISBN: 1-949716-55-4
ISBN-13: 978-1-949716-55-9

Cover design and Typesetting by
Rachel Rosales, Orange Peal Design

TABLE OF CONTENTS

Volume Introduction   i
Joshua Benjamins

Thirteenth Chapter: On the providence of God

1	Providence Is Defined	1
2	Preliminary Objections to Providence Are Answered	5
3	On Providence, Necessity, and Contingency	11
4	Providence Exists and Involves Power as Well as Knowledge	17
5	Nothing Is Exempt from Providence	25
6	Providence Is Immutable and Does Not Preclude Contingency	33

Fourteenth Chapter: Whether God is the author of sin

1	Arguments that God Is Not the Cause of Sin	45
2	Arguments that God Is the Cause of Sin	51
3	A Solution Is Proposed	59
4	Three Types of Divine Actions	63
5	God Is Not the Efficient Cause of Sin	75
6	God Suggests Things that Men Take as Occasions to Sin	79
7	God Permits Sin, But This Permission Involves Will	83
8	The Deformity of Sin Inheres in the Will	91
9	Sins Can Be Punishments for Other Sins	99
10	The Causes of Sin Summarized	103
11	Arguments that God Is Not the Cause of Sin Are Answered	105
12	Arguments that God Is the Cause of Sin Are Answered	117
13	In What Sense the Will Is Free	135
14	In What Sense Sin Is Part of God's Will	139

15	God's Twofold Will	145
16	Conforming Ourselves to God's Will	159

Fifteenth Chapter:
In what sense God is said to repent and to tempt — 165

1	What It Means for God to Repent	167
2	Why and How God Tempts Men	175
3	Whether We Should Pray to Be Spared Temptation	181
	Bibliography	185
	Index	193

VOLUME INTRODUCTION
Joshua Benjamins

This volume contains a translation of three of the *Loci Communes* ("Common Places") of Peter Martyr Vermigli (1499–1562), dealing respectively with the providence of God, God's authorship of sin, and the sense in which God is said to repent and to tempt. Born in Florence and educated at the University of Padua, Peter Martyr ranks among the theological giants of the sixteenth century. Regius Professor of Divinity at Oxford, prolific biblical commentator, and penetrating theologian, he was also a friend of John Calvin, confidant of Thomas Cranmer, and companion of Heinrich Bullinger. His influence extended far beyond his native Italy to the farthest corners of Christian Europe. To cite but one indication of his popularity, his works went through 110 separate printings in the century from 1550 to 1650.[1] Joseph Justus Scaliger (1540–1609), one of his Protestant contemporaries, remarked that "the two most excellent theologians of our time are John Calvin and Peter Martyr."[2] The English church historian John

---

1. John Patrick Donnelly, *Calvinism and Scholasticism in Vermigli's Doctrine of Man and Grace* (Leiden: Brill, 1976), 3.

2. Gordon Huelin, "Peter Martyr and the English Reformation" (Ph.D. dissertation, University of London, 1954), 178.

Strype (1643–1737) considered him "worthy to be mentioned with Melancthon [*sic*] and Calvin."³ A vigorous force behind the abortive Italian Reformation and afterward, with greater success, behind the English Reformation, Vermigli wrought a synthesis of scholasticism with Reformed theology that had significant import for the future shape of Reformed thought.

The *Loci Communes* consists of scholia on a range of theological topics, extracted from throughout Vermigli's biblical commentaries.⁴ They were gathered and published in London in 1576, fourteen years after his death, by the French minister Robert Masson. Republished a dozen times over the decades that followed, Vermigli's *Loci* enjoyed tremendous popularity and did much to further their author's later reputation as a premier systematizer of Reformed theology. The chapters translated here illustrate some of the defining characteristics of Vermigli's theology. In sketching his doctrine of providence, causality, and free will, the Reformer of Italy produced a fertile and creative synthesis that combined scriptural interpretation with insights from both theological and philosophical sources, supplemented by philological expertise and rhetorical strategies drawn from his humanistic training.

After a brief analysis of Peter Martyr's definition of providence, this introduction explains how these three

---

3. John Strype, *Memorials of the Most Reverend Father in God Thomas Cranmer* . . . (London: George Routledge and Co., 1853), 2:164.

4. On the history of the *Loci Communes*, see Joseph McLelland, "A Literary History of the Loci Communes," in *A Companion to Peter Martyr Vermigli*, ed. W. J. Torrance Kirby, Emidio Campi, and Frank A. James III (Leiden: Brill, 2009), 479–94.

loci, in dialogue with earlier philosophers and theologians, attempt to clarify two major issues in ancient and medieval debates on providence: first, the relationship between fate, chance, contingency, and providence; and secondly, the sense in which God is the cause of evil. The following section probes the ways in which Vermigli integrates and authoritatively cites the various categories of sources—ancient, biblical, patristic, medieval, contemporary—whose confluence is visible in this section of the *Loci Communes*. It also highlights some of the humanist features of his exposition, particularly his philological expertise and his use of illustrative similes. A final section surveys the textual basis, citational practice, and goals of the present translation and accompanying notes.

Vermigli's Definition of Providence

In good scholastic fashion, Vermigli begins his discussion of providence with a definition: providence is "the system [*ratio*] which God uses in directing things toward their proper ends" (13 section 1). A little later, he offers a similar definition: "a power or faculty of God by which he directs all things and conducts them to their proper ends" (13 section 7). Both formulations recall Aquinas's definition of providence as "the relation [*ratio*] of things ordered toward their end" which preexists in the divine mind.[5] Etymologically, the Latin term *providentia* suggests seeing something before it happens, and in this sense it can be synonymous with foreknowledge. Alternatively, as Mikko Posti notes,

---

5. Thomas Aquinas, *Summa Theologiae* 1ᵃ q. 22 a. 1 co., cited in Mikko Posti, *Medieval Theories of Divine Providence 1250–1350* (Leiden: Brill, 2020), 80. On the term *ratio*, see note 4 on p.2 below.

a distinction could be made between the prefixes *pro-* and *prae-*, such that the latter means foreknowledge and the former carries a causal connotation (to see on behalf of something).⁶ For Vermigli, providence entails much more than simply advance knowledge. It is crucial for his analysis that providence is a species in the genus of power (see the second definition above). Providence thus includes not only knowledge but also God's effectual will in fixing events, together with the power to direct and govern all things (13 sections 1, 5, 7). Insofar as providence comes under God's will and knowledge, both of which pertain to his essence, it is immutable (13 section 12). If providence includes will and power, it is wrong to construe it as mere foreknowledge, as though God simply brings things to the point where human beings can choose or reject them (13 section 15). Foreknowledge, Vermigli argues, is preceded by will: "God is able to foreknow only those future things which are going to take place" (14 section 32).

Vermigli's doctrine of providence is closely connected to and flows from his doctrine of creation. God not only brings things into being, but also sustains, governs, and directs all things once they have been created: without the operation of his providence, they would collapse (13 section 7). Anything that escaped providence would *ipso facto* be outside creation as well (13 section 8). As Silvianne Aspray comments, "it is therefore the doctrine of creation which leads Peter Martyr to stress the unity of God's providential workings in the world."⁷ God does not

---

6. Posti, *Medieval Theories of Divine Providence*, 49.

7. Silvianne Aspray, *Metaphysics in the Reformation: The Case of Peter*

sit idly in a watchtower giving loose reins to the world (14 section 41). Vermigli consequently rejects the theory that God's "guidance merely consists in his supplying a common influence to all things, which individual things draw to themselves" (13 section 7).

Vermigli's explication of God's providence focuses largely on two problems, which the following sections of this introduction will consider in some detail. They are, respectively, the relationship that providence bears to fate, chance, and contingency, and the sense in which God is to be considered the cause of evil, particularly sin. The strategies Vermigli uses to solve these notoriously knotty problems reflect his deep familiarity with the ancient and medieval philosophical tradition in its full breadth.

Fate, Chance, Contingency, and Providence

The first major issue which Vermigli confronts in these chapters is the way in which divine providence relates to fate, chance or fortune, and contingency. In brief, if God's will functions as the essential cause of all existing things, is any room left for chance events? If God foreordains everything that comes to pass, what space remains for contingency in the affairs of the world? Do secondary causes have any genuine function? These questions played a crucial role in both ancient and medieval discussions of providence, and Vermigli avails himself of a long lineage of theoretical reflection on such issues, Christian as well as non-Christian. To appreciate his intervention, it will be useful to briefly survey the theories of providence offered

---

Martyr Vermigli (Oxford: The British Academy, 2021), 31.

by Aristotle and later Peripatetics, the Stoics, the Neoplatonists, Augustine, and Thomas Aquinas, who together represent the major interlocutors and influences for Vermigli's own teaching.

While most interpreters do not find in Aristotle (384–322 BC) the idea of a God who exercises personal, providential care, Aristotle does speak of a First Cause, or unmoved mover, who is responsible for the universe's order.[8] This God is pure act, simple and immutable. Although Aristotle lacks a doctrine of personal providence, the theory of chance and accidental causality that he articulated exercised a great influence on Christian theology from the Middle Ages onward. Aristotle discusses chance (τύχη) in *Physics* 11.4–6, where he construes it as an accidental (*per accidens*), as opposed to an essential (*per se*), cause of events. For Aristotle, there are genuinely chance events in the world that lack a *per se* cause. He gives the example of a man who goes to the market with some other purpose in view, but ends up collecting a debt by luck. This acknowledgement of chance events crucially enables Aristotelian natural philosophy to avoid falling into determinism. Accidental causation, in Aristotle's theory, "follows from the fact that most causes do not always cause their proper effects but only do so in most cases."[9]

The Peripatetic school founded by Aristotle sought to clarify the Philosopher's doctrine of providence. The early Peripatetics were generally of the opinion that divine providence only applies to the spheres above the moon, while

---

8. Aristotle, *Metaphysics* 12.10.1075a15–23.

9. Posti, *Medieval Theories of Divine Providence*, 20.

the sublunary realm is devoid of intentional providential control. However, in the third century AD, the Peripatetic philosopher Alexander of Aphrodisias, in a treatise entitled *On Fate*, argued that divine providence operates through the mediation of the heavenly bodies and through them extends to the sublunary world. For Alexander, providence is not concerned with individual beings but only with the continued existence of sublunary *species* of beings. This stipulation was intended to solve the problem of "how the divine can attend simultaneously to a multiplicity of details and over the injustices suffered by some particular individuals."[10] Alexander's Aristotelian doctrine of providence, which conceived of divine providence exclusively as a final cause rather than an efficient cause, was transmitted to the Western world through Averroes and was taught in the universities.[11]

In contrast to Aristotle and the Peripatetics, the Stoics embraced causal determinism: all events are connected in an unbroken chain of causes. The Stoics equated this series of causes with "fate" (εἱμαρμένη) and also with providence: everything that happens according to fate also happens according to providence, since the immanent power of God—conceived by the Stoics as a craftsmanlike fire—infuses all of material reality. For the Stoics, the existence of fate was confirmed by the obvious organic unity of the world as well as the success of divination. Their deterministic picture left no room for contingent or chance events:

---

10. R. W. Sharples, "Alexander of Aphrodisias on Divine Providence: Two Problems," *Classical Quarterly* 32, no. 1 (1982): 198.

11. Posti, *Medieval Theories of Divine Providence*, 33, 54.

everything that happens in the world is predetermined. Nevertheless, the Stoics also held to the compatibilist position that human will can be reconciled with causal determinism. Even though human choices and behaviors are causally determined, this is compatible with our actions being "up to us" (ἐφ' ἡμῖν), since they are determined by our own perceptions and ensuing choices. As Posti notes, the Stoic position was routinely criticized in the Middle Ages for its determinism, yet it "remained highly influential as the shared enemy of the Platonist and Peripatetic schools."[12]

The Neoplatonists rejected both the Peripatetic theory, which denied any providence over individuals, and the Stoic theory, which equated providence with an ineluctably fated chain of causes. They worried that each of these views would undermine human freedom and moral responsibility. Plotinus (204/5–270 AD), the founder of Neoplatonism, equated providence with Intellect, the emanation from the One. He widened its purview to include all sublunary things, including the actions of rational agents, and extended it to miniscule details of the world, which the Peripatetics had excluded from divine knowledge.[13] Proclus (412–485 AD), a long-time head of Plato's Athenian Academy, drew a distinction between fate and providence: providence (πρόνοια) is divine, the benevolent activity of the First Principle, while fate (εἱμαρμένη), which depends on providence, is confined to natural and physical things. The Neoplatonic theory pro-

---

12. Posti, *Medieval Theories of Divine Providence*, 26.

13. Posti, *Medieval Theories of Divine Providence*, 36–37.

foundly shaped the thought of both Augustine and Boethius, two of the most influential expositors of providence for the medieval period.

Augustine of Hippo (354–430 AD) wrestled throughout his writings with questions concerning providence, free will, and the cause of evil. He maintained the Christian (and Platonist) conviction that God is good, but also stressed God's omnipotence and the absence of any weakness or imperfection in the supreme Being. For Augustine, nothing in the natural world can lie outside of the order of providence. In Book 5 of *City of God*, he denies that anything happens by fate. He grants that there is a fixed sequence of causes in God (which is only improperly called "fate"), yet holds that human will is not meaningless on that account, since the will is itself contained in the sequence of causes that God has determined. Augustine also refutes Cicero's arguments against God's foreknowledge of future events, based on the premise that divine foreknowledge cannot be reconciled with human freedom.[14] Even though all events are foreknown by God, human volitions are efficient causes of human actions. Augustine thus maintains the genuine character of free will alongside the authenticity of God's foreknowledge and sovereignty. As he rejected fate as an independent causal agent, Augustine also rejected chance, viewing it as a threat to God's all-embracing providential government: "Whatever happens by chance happens without design. Whatever happens without design does not happen due to Providence. If therefore

---

14. Augustine, *De civitate dei* 5.9.

some things in the world happen by chance, then not all the world is governed by Providence."[15]

Thomas Aquinas (1225–1274 AD) addressed the interlocking issues of fate, chance, fortune, and providence in numerous places. Like the Neoplatonists and Augustine, he maintains the radical, unceasing dependence of all created things on God as the supreme cause, and affirms that all things without exception are subject to God's providence. Also like Augustine, Aquinas understands providence to be the execution in time of God's intellectual cognition of order. In line with Augustine's critique of the concept of fate, Aquinas "prefers to speak of the execution of providence as governance (*gubernatio*) rather than fate" and "is reluctant to admit the existence of fate, understood as a cause, in any other sense than the will and power of God."[16] However, Aquinas also affirms the real existence of secondary causes in the world, and holds that not all of these causes bear a necessary connection to their effects. Some *per se* causes do not produce their effects in all cases, and chance events transpire when a *per se* cause issues in something other than the typical outcome. Events of this sort do not have a proper *per se* cause, but merely an accidental cause. Thus, Aquinas follows Aristotle in defining chance and fortune "as causes that create their effects beyond the intention of agents acting towards an end."[17] This account of chance events enables Aquinas,

---

15. Augustine, *De diversis quaestionibus octoginta tribus* 24 (*Eighty-Three Different Questions*, 50).

16. Posti, *Medieval Theories of Divine Providence*, 80.

17. Posti, *Medieval Theories of Divine Providence*, 81.

like Aristotle, to avoid causal determinism. For Aquinas, secondary causes are responsible for the contingent character of certain events that are produced by the joint operation of God and his creatures. Scholars have referred to Aquinas's doctrine as "providential determinism"—the view that "the effects of all the lower causes, including the actions of human free will, are predetermined from the viewpoint of the infallible divine providence."[18]

Vermigli seeks to untangle the nexus of fortune, fate, providence, and contingency in *locus* 13, entitled "On Providence," a scholium from the lectures on Genesis which he delivered at Strasbourg around 1545–1546. First, he follows the lead of Aquinas (who in turn had followed Aristotle) in conceptualizing chance and fortune as causes that bring about their effects beyond, or contrary to, the will of an agent, such that "something happens that is not intended or decided or resolved, contrary to expectation and when we are unawares" (13 section 4). Vermigli upholds the reality of fortune in this sense, and sees it as posing no hindrance to divine providence, since events that occur fortuitously from a human perspective nevertheless occur through God's foreknowledge and awareness. He illustrates this point with a simile taken from Aquinas's *Summa Theologiae*: if a master sends two servants to the same place, the meeting of the two servants happens by chance with regard to themselves, but is directly intended if compared to the master who ordered it. The existence of so-called chance events reflects the limitations of the human intellect in grasping the interrelation of causes and

---

18. Posti, *Medieval Theories of Divine Providence*, 90.

effects, rather than manifesting some independent controlling power in the world.

Secondly, Vermigli expressly rejects the Peripatetic thesis—a version of which Averroes had later defended as well—that providence extends only as far as the sphere of the moon, since the divine would not concern itself with sublunary things (13 section 7). This stratagem aimed to safeguard the nobility of providence, but unduly limited its scope in the process. The Peripatetic view flies in the face of Scripture's teaching that even the most mundane aspects of human affairs are matters of concern to God and come under his providential arrangement.

Third, Vermigli distinguishes his doctrine of providence from the causal determinism of Stoic philosophy, which equated providence with fate, namely, the chain of causes (*connexio causarum*) that unravels in a fully determined manner. Vermigli anticipates that his readers may suspect a revival of the Stoic opinion in his claim that, while things are contingent of their own nature, they are necessary if referred to God's providence. Following the lead of Augustine in Book 5 of *City of God*,[19] Vermigli is willing to reluctantly tolerate the term "fate" if it be understood as a synonym for the providential will of God, but he rejects the Stoic teaching that (on his reading) would make fate to rule even over God himself (13 section 8).

Finally, on the issue of providence and contingency, Vermigli's position is fully consonant with that of Aquinas. He insists that God's providence does not eliminate contingency in mundane affairs, since created things retain their individual natures and inherent properties. "All

---

19. Augustine, *De civitate dei* 5.9.

things are necessary if they be referred to God's providence, but of their own nature they are contingent" (13 section 16). Events are contingent "'in themselves" (13 section 14), that is, as far as their proximate causes are concerned (13 section 4), but they are necessary if we refer them to God who inclines them in one direction rather than another (13 section 14). Moreover, although there is an element of necessity in God's decree, there is equally an element of contingency in God's determining of the act (13 section 4). Here we glimpse one of Vermigli's core principles, consonant with medieval scholasticism's respect for nature: God does not violate the natures of things (13 section 14). Peter Martyr thus upholds the reality and meaningfulness of secondary causes, even while making such causes instruments of God's providence (13 section 11). God does not act by the immediate (that is, unmediated) exercise of his sovereign power. Instead, he brings about the outcomes which he has decreed through means such as admonitions, speeches, and rebukes (13 section 16), and such means "are not applied in vain" (14 section 26).

The Cause of Sin

The second major issue confronting any expositor of providence is the so-called problem of evil. Although this epistemic question can embrace evil of all types, including deformity, suffering, death, and natural calamities, the *Loci Communes* focuses squarely on moral evil, that is, sin. The entirety of Vermigli's long fourteenth *locus* is devoted to the question of whether God is, properly speaking, the cause of sin. Peter Martyr first addressed this problem during the Oxford phase of his career (1547–1549) while lecturing on the Letter to the Romans, and he returned to it repeatedly in later biblical commentaries.[20] His most thorough treatment of God's authorship of sin came in the Samuel commentary which he composed in Zurich (1556–1562), where he devoted two separate scholia to the topic; together, these comprise the bulk of *locus* 14. Vermigli's carefully qualified answer to the question consists essentially in two theses, laid out early in the discussion: "first, that God is not the cause of sin through himself (*per se*) and properly; second, that nothing happens in the world, not even sins themselves, apart from his will and choice or providence" (14 chapter 6, restated in chapter 37). Since the period of the early Church, orthodox Christianity had consistently affirmed each of these tenets. The problem, of course, lay in how the two could be harmonized with one another. Peter Martyr's solution rests on a number of different strategies, weaving together independent strands from various philosophical and theological traditions.

The first strand, which lies at the heart of Vermigli's solution, has its origin in Augustinian metaphysics. Augustine stressed the inherent goodness of creation. All creatures, having been brought into being from nothing (*ex nihilo*), are sustained in their existence by the power and goodness of God, which prevent them from returning again to nothingness. Being as such is a good, since it involves participation in the God who is supreme being and supreme goodness. Conversely, evil as such has

---

20. Donnelly, *Calvinism and Scholasticism in Vermigli's Doctrine of Man and Grace*, 117.

no ontological existence; it is nothing but the privation of goodness. Hence, it is illogical to fault God for creating it.

Vermigli approves of this basic solution, but further refines it using the categories of Aristotelian scholasticism. Evil is the privation of a *habitus*, that is, of "a good...that is required for the perfection of any creature" (14 section 6). Evil cannot subsist apart from a subject, and that subject, *qua* nature, is a good thing. The specific good in which sin subsists is human action. Human action is a good thing in itself, for every action "depends on the principle of all things," namely God (14 section 3). The act in which sin inheres is therefore truly existent and good. But sin, as privation, "deprives human action of seemliness and of obedience to the word of God" (14 section 6).

The second strand in Vermigli's answer consists in a careful discrimination of efficient and non-efficient causality. As adumbrated in the first of his two theses, "God is not the cause of sin through himself and properly." In the language of Aristotelian causality, God is not the efficient cause of sin, *efficient cause* referring to the source of a particular change or motion. The subject in which sin inheres, namely human action, does have God as its efficient cause, insofar as it entails something positive (14 section 19). But of sin itself God cannot properly be called the efficient cause (14 section 12). Sin, after all, is an evil, and evils, as privations, have no efficient causes. They possess only "deficient causes"—an expression coined by Augustine to describe a lack or "deficiency in the willing of something by an otherwise good agent."[21] Augustine remarked, to seek

---

21. Richard A. Muller, *Dictionary of Latin and Greek Theological Terms* (Grand Rapids: Baker House, 1985), s.v. "causa deficiens."

knowledge of such a cause would be "as if someone sought to see darkness, or hear silence."[22]

From this conception of sin as a privation that has only a deficient cause, it follows that God is not the efficient cause, or "true cause," of sin. Yet Vermigli affirms that he is "the cause in some sense" (14 section 7). More specifically, adopting the language of Aquinas, he describes God as "the cause that removes the obstacle," or in Latin *causa removens prohibens*. As soon as God withdraws the grace and power that uphold human beings in existence, their sinful will inclines of itself to evil. Following Augustine, Vermigli conceives of sin as the motion of turning away from God to non-being. He writes that "this motion of turning away from God, since it falls short and deprives human actions of the appropriate goodness, does indeed have a cause, but a deficient one" (14 section 17). Insofar as sin has a definable cause, then, it is an inward cause: man's corrupt nature, his depraved affections and inclinations (14 sections 9, 12, 29).

There is a further sense in which God is a non-efficient cause of sin, namely insofar as he rules and governs sins. This means, first, that he directs the manner in which sin occurs. Although the cause of sin lies in human beings, the power of God determines at what time and upon whom they break forth (13 section 11; 14 section 16). God regulates the circumstances of sin "in regard to time, manner, type, matter, such that it is bent now against this man, now against that one" (14 sections 12–13). Secondly, as we will see below, God causes sin to serve his own good purposes.

---

22. Augustine, *De civitate dei* 12.7 (*City of God*, NPNF 1/2:230).

A third and closely related strand in Vermigli's exposition concerns the crucial distinction between primary and secondary causality. God is the cause of all things, but "lower things receive the motion of the first cause in keeping with their nature" (14 section 21). God as the highest cause concurs in human actions, but it is sinful men themselves, performing acts of evil, who are the "proximate causes" of sin (14 section 10), and it is from the proximate cause that the fault is incurred. God's will concurs indirectly in bad things, yet it is not, strictly speaking, a cause of such things: "sin does not properly fall under the will of God" (14 section 16), because it has no efficient cause.

When combined with a metaphysical schema in which evil is merely privation, the distinction between primary and secondary causality enables Peter Martyr to avoid the conclusion that God, as the supreme cause, bears the guilt for moral evil. As Silvianne Aspray puts it, the secondary causes do not "'introduce' anything which has an independent ontological standing. Rather, whatever is 'added' is privative."[23] Vermigli stresses the asymmetry between the contribution that God makes to acts of evil and the contribution of human will: the work proceeds from each "in a very different way and by a different reason" (14 section 10; cf. 15 section 6). God, the primary cause, directs sins so as to fulfill and effect his plans, whereas sinners, the secondary causes, willingly comply with their own lusts (14 section 9). Thus, "he justly wills what he wills; those who sin unjustly will what they will" (14 section 16). As Aspray has emphasized, Vermigli's model of human action, on which neither the human will nor God can be

---

23. Aspray, *Metaphysics in the Reformation*, 33.

called the full cause (*causa tota*) of any action, "attempts to steer a middle ground between an understanding that divine agency is overridden by human agency, on the one hand, and the notion that human agency is obliterated by divine agency, on the other."[24]

Sin thus has no efficient cause, but it has human will, turning away from God and thus from being, as a deficient cause. There are other, more remote causes of sin as well. In 14 section 24, Vermigli enumerates sin's diverse causes in sequence: "the cause of sin is human will, intellect, depraved affections, the sensitive appetite, the apparent good which presents itself…the tinder of original sin…weakness, ignorance, the suggestion of the devil, the suggestion of evil men…bad examples." The devil (like evil men) is an imperfect rather than a sufficient cause: he makes suggestions, but "cannot induce the will to commit sin of necessity" (14 section 12). Apart from the suggestions of the devil and evil men, Vermigli also confronts the idea that God generates suggestions to sin. He argues that God presents to the human mind considerations that are good in themselves, but that become stumbling blocks due to people's corrupted nature: they take these suggestions in an evil direction such that they become occasions for committing sin. Such suggestions "cannot properly be called causes of sin," but merely occasions: it is only because of mankind's inner depravity that they issue in evil actions (14 section 13). This principle guides the analysis of *locus* 15, where Vermigli tackles the question of wheth-

---

24. Aspray, *Metaphysics in the Reformation*, 34. See also Donnelly, *Calvinism and Scholasticism in Vermigli's Doctrine of Man and Grace*, 120.

er God tempts men to sin. His answer is that God does indeed tempt men, but does so for righteous ends: on the one hand, to punish the wicked and render them further liable to judgment, thus manifesting his justice; on the other, to increase the virtues of the upright, to prove their value, and to make them more conscious of God's favor and mercy (15 section 5).

The complicated assignment of sin's causality brings us to a fourth strand in the tapestry of Vermigli's analysis, namely the distinctions that he posits within the divine will. In line with Augustine, Vermigli asserts that the will of God is the cause of all things. He is aware of the debate in medieval scholasticism about the relative priority of intellect or will in God, but declines to pass a verdict in the dispute, referring his reader instead to Scotus and Aquinas (13 section 7). Following scholastic usage, Vermigli discriminates between two sorts of will in God, the *will of the sign* and the *will of good pleasure* (14 section 38). The former "consists in the law, commands, promises, threats, and counsels." The latter, the will of good pleasure, is the mighty and effectual will which no creature can resist; this will remains hidden and secret in God. By the will of the sign, God wills that all human beings observe his precepts and attain to eternal life; but it is his efficacious will—the will of good pleasure—"that rules and governs man's wicked desires and sins and that gives man over to his own perversity."[25] Vermigli is at pains to clarify that these are not two separate faculties within God; he maintains firmly that God has only one will (14 section 2),

---

25. Donnelly, *Calvinism and Scholasticism in Vermigli's Doctrine of Man and Grace*, 122

but recognizes that this will is manifold in respect to its objects (14 section 26).

To the distinction between the will of the sign and the will of good pleasure, Vermigli adds a second distinction: God has one will which is secret, another which is open or revealed (15 section 3). This distinction has important practical consequences for human action: "human will must be conformed to the will of God in some way.... Yet it is not necessary that what God wills to happen be pleasing to us in all ways" (14 section 43). We should regulate our actions and affections according to God's revealed will rather than according to his decretive will or good pleasure. This means distinguishing what accords with God's will and what accords with our own. As Richard Muller puts it, for Vermigli "the partial revelation of the divine will does not always yield the acquiescence that would follow the full revelation, but the failure to acquiesce fully is not sinful" when one is following the commands of the will of the sign.[26] In Vermigli's nuanced and pastorally sensitive explanation of this point, one glimpses his high view of the integrity of human nature: "what things agree with our nature we will discern from its constitution, that is, from the law of nature and of God, but sometimes also from an inward inspiration of the Spirit" (14 section 43).

A similar distinction can be drawn between God's effective will and his permissive will. The Syrian theologian John of Damascus (c.675–749 AD) had contrasted God's

---

26. Richard Muller, *Post-Reformation Reformed Dogmatics: The Rise and Development of Reformed Orthodoxy, ca. 1520 to ca. 1725*, vol. 3: *The Divine Essence and Attributes* (Grand Rapids: Baker Academic, 2003), 441.

antecedent will of good pleasure with his consequent will of permission, and Aquinas had later adopted this distinction.[27] Vermigli cites John's distinction, without disapproval, in 14 section 36. However, the bare notion of permission does not carry sufficient explanatory power, in Vermigli's eyes. God's orchestration of sin does involve permission, but permission itself is "a certain type of will," albeit "not efficient will" (14 section 16). He repeatedly quotes Augustine's statement (in *Enchiridion* 100) that God permits either unwillingly or willingly; clearly not unwillingly, therefore willingly. Vermigli concludes, "God not only permits but also, in some fixed way, wills sin—yet not insofar as it is sin, seeing that of necessity his will always inclines toward the good, but insofar as it is a punishment for earlier deeds of wickedness" (14 section 40).

A fifth and final strand in Vermigli's doctrine consists in the positive purposes that evil serves. Mikko Posti, in his thorough survey of medieval discussions of providence, has distinguished two strategies for explaining moral evil: an accidental strategy, which holds that God preserves intact the nature of his rational creatures (including free choice) because of their inherent value for the created order, and an instrumental strategy, which holds that created evils do form part of God's providential plan and are grounded in his recognition that certain goods could not be attained without some evils.[28] When Vermigli contends that the defect of sin originated in "the free choice of Adam, whom God had created whole, free, and complete,

---

27. Posti, *Medieval Theories of Divine Providence*, 52.

28. Posti, *Medieval Theories of Divine Providence*, 57 et passim.

yet not in such a way that he could not fall" (14 section 42), this argument represent an accidental strategy, in Posti's terms. However, the instrumental strategy, stressing that evils maximize the goodness of the world-order, also finds expression in these chapters of the *Loci Communes*. This type of argument goes back to Augustine, who in a famous statement quoted by Vermigli asserted that God, being omnipotent, is able to bring about good even from evil,[29] and understood God's intention to be that "His unmerited mercy should shine forth the more brightly in contrast with the unworthiness of its objects."[30] Aquinas, too, had argued that certain goods, such as the perseverance and patience of the martyrs, could not be realized without evil.[31]

In line with Augustine and Aquinas, Vermigli stresses the ways that God uses sins to serve good ends. They manifest divine justice and mercy and promote the order of the cosmos (13 section 4; 14 section 25). They provide scope for showing the endurance of the martyrs, thus displaying God's goodness as well as his might and power (13 section 9). Moreover, by using perverted wills for his own good purposes, God exhibits wisdom and power in his ability to accomplish his ends either mediately or immediately (14 section 12). Finally, sins also serve God's good purposes in their function as punishments for other sins (14 section 6, 22).

---

29. Augustine, *Enchiridion* 11 (*Enchiridion*, NPNF 1/3:240).

30. Augustine, *Enchiridion* 27 (*Enchiridion*, NPNF 1/3:246); cf. *De civitate dei* 11.18, 23.

31. Aquinas, *Summa contra Gentiles* l. 3 cap. 71 n. 6.

Vermigli neatly sums up his multifaceted answer to the cause of sin as follows: "Hence, we conclude that the actions themselves, that is, the subjects of sins, are from God, and that he himself withdraws his grace and help when it seems good to him; moreover, he rules and bends people's depraved lusts wherever it pleases him. And since he utilizes people's sins for the punishments of other sins, it cannot be said that he did not will them in any way" (14 section 42).

Vermigli's Interlocutors and Influences

The breadth of Vermigli's learning and education finds ample expression in the wide range of sources which he quotes and discusses in the *loci* on providence and the cause of sin. Broadly speaking, these *fontes* fall into five groups: classical authors, scriptural writers, patristic sources, medieval philosophers and theologians, and Protestant Reformers.

The *loci* are studded with quotations taken from ancient Greek and Roman sources, reflecting the author's erudite command of classical literature. Verses from the ancient poets—Hesiod, Horace, Juvenal, Ovid—make occasional appearances, either as foils for Vermigli's propositions or as corroborators of their truth. Among the philosophers, Plato is subjected to criticism for removing evils from the purview of divine providence and for denying that God ever appears in human form (14 section 35), as well as for a creation myth that severs the distribution of good qualities to mankind from that of evil qualities (13 section 2); yet Vermigli commends him for upholding the perfection of God's knowledge (13 section

3). As for Cicero, his eloquent tribute to a supernaturally well-orchestrated universe is quoted as proof that unaided natural reason is able to discern divine providence (13 section 1), although Vermigli unsurprisingly censures the Stoic position on fate and free will that Cicero articulates (13 section 8).[32] Aristotle is undoubtedly Vermigli's most important philosophical influence among the ancients. These *loci* evince the deep knowledge of the Philosopher which is most clearly visible in Vermigli's commentary on the *Nicomachean Ethics*. Aristotle is an important source for Vermigli's discussion of fortuitous events (13 section 11), and Vermigli makes heavy use of terms, concepts, and categories stemming from the Stagirite's logical works and the *Metaphysics*.

In contrast to the author's occasional references to secular literature, citations from Scripture are pervasive, numbering in the hundreds in these three *loci* alone. The primacy of Scripture in Peter Martyr's exposition reflects both his high regard for the authority of the Bible and the original publication context of the *loci*, where they formed part of his exegetical practice, as "additional explanations of the biblical text."[33] Vermigli's scriptural citations come from all parts of the canon. He also quotes non-canonical books on occasion, albeit with the caveat that such works do not carry the same authority as canonical Scripture (13 sections 7, 10).

---

32. See Donnelly, *Calvinism and Scholasticism in Vermigli's Doctrine of Man and Grace*, 143.

33. Frank A. James III, ed. and trans., *Predestination and Justification: Two Theological Loci* (Kirksville, MO: Truman State University Press, 2003), xxii.

The way in which Vermigli interprets these passages, and in which he erects a theological edifice upon their foundations, is unmistakeably shaped by the patristic tradition. In these *loci*, as in many others, it is Augustine of Hippo who exercises paramount influence among the Church Fathers. As detailed above, the main lineaments of Vermigli's teachings on providence and the cause of sin derive largely from Augustine's writings, especially the *Enchiridion*. Augustine is quoted some thirty times in these *loci*, with a few especially important quotations being repeated twice or thrice. Other patristic authors play supporting roles, sometimes ambivalent ones. Origen and Cyril are criticized for making foreknowledge an explanatory cause of events (13 section 15). Anselm and Jerome are both cited with approbation on several occasions, the latter in particular for his exegetical insights. On the other hand, John of Damascus is roundly criticized for his unorthodox claim that τὰ ἐφ' ἡμῖν ("the things that depend on us") not only belong to human free will but are entirely outside the boundaries of divine providence. Vermigli approves Damascene's distinction between permission and good pleasure, but dismisses his distinction between an antecedent and a following volition in God, on the grounds that it undermines the unity of the divine will (14 section 36).

As indicated above, Peter Martyr's discussions here are deeply indebted to the Middle Age's rich heritage of reflection on questions of fate, chance, causality, and providence. Although he does not blindly follow the doctrines of the Peripatetic school, Aristotelian scholasticism—often mediated through Aquinas—furnishes him with both terminology and metaphysical principles. The *loci* on providence provide many examples of the "basic Aristotelian substructure" that John Patrick Donnelly has identified in the thought of this Reformer.[34] Vermigli's categories of contingency come from the Aristotelian tradition; so too does the specification of matter and will as contingency's twofold foundation (13 section 5). His definition of providence is couched in terms of Aristotle's four causes (13 section 7). From Aristotle, too, comes the important distinction between absolute, or simple, and hypothetical necessity (13 sections 4, 13). Vermigli draws readily on philosophical maxims taught in the schools, such as "If active things be fitted to passive things, a necessary action follows" (13 section 10), and "Every accidental cause should be referred to an essential one" (13 section 11)—the latter a key plank in Aquinas's analysis of causality. Aquinas supplies Vermigli also with the terminology of *causa removens prohibens*, "a cause that removes the obstacle" (14 sections 7, 30).[35] Similarly, the scholastic distinction between the will of good sign and the will of good pleasure is developed in 14 section 38.

---

34. Donnelly, *Calvinism and Scholasticism in Vermigli's Doctrine of Man and Grace*, 29n.58.

35. Marvin Anderson criticizes Donnelly's contention that *causa removens prohibens* is an example of scholastic influence in the Samuel commentary, on the grounds that "the concept of privation is Augustinian and not scholastic." "Peter Martyr Vermigli: Protestant Humanist," in *Peter Martyr Vermigli and Italian Reform*, ed. Joseph C. McLelland (Waterloo, ON: Wilfred Laurier University Press, 1980), 75. Anderson's dichotomy here is unhelpful. While it is true that Peter Martyr's use of privation and deficiency can be traced back to Augustine's Neoplatonism, those concepts themselves came to be filtered through Thomistic metaphysics, and in this case, Vermigli's Thomistic vocabulary points precisely to the confluence of Augustinian Neoplatonism and Thomistic Aristotelianism in his doctrine of providence.

Among Vermigli's fellow Protestant Reformers, it is Ulrich Zwingli who is quoted most often in these pages, especially for his sermon *On the Providence of God* (14 sections 14, 32–33), although the degree of Zwinglian influence on Vermigli's treatment has been questioned.[36] Zwingli and Luther are together referred to in highly complimentary terms as "those heroes of the Reformed faith" (14 section 37). Alongside these two theological heavyweights, Oecolampadius, Bucer, and Calvin receive brief mention in the same paragraph as adherents of Vermigli's position on free will. As for Philip Melanchthon, "that venerable man, whom I love and accept," Vermigli anticipates that readers will detect a rift between the two men's positions on free will, and strains to obviate any perceived dissonance by directing his readers to the earlier editions of Melanchthon's *Loci Communes*, an important early model for the commonplace genre.[37]

If the scholasticism of the schools is a pervasive influence on the vocabulary and philosophical marrow of the *loci*, Vermigli's work is also shaped by humanistic influences. As N. Scott Amos has argued, Vermigli's *loci*-centered approach to scriptural exposition, which takes individual passages as occasions for extended theological discussions, bears the imprint of sixteenth-century biblical human-

---

36. Donnelly, *Calvinism and Scholasticism in Vermigli's Doctrine of Man and Grace*, 118n.64; see also 128–29 for Vermigli's engagement with Zwingli's *On Providence*.

37. On the difference in approach between Melanchthon's *loci* and Vermigli's, see N. Scott Amos, "Exegesis and Theological Method," in Torrance et al., *Companion to Peter Martyr Vermigli*, 175–93.

ism.[38] On the more granular level, one of the features of Vermigli's humanist training amply illustrated in this selection is his philological expertise, including a familiarity with the Hebrew language and with rabbinic tradition.[39] For instance, he mentions the derivation, from the verb *hisgiah*, of the Hebrew word for providence, *hashgachah*, a key term in rabbinic literature (13 section 1). Elsewhere, interpreting the scriptural passages which refer to God's permission, he resorts to the "Hebrew truth" (*Hebraica veritas*) and interrogates the Hebrew verb *schillach* by collating its various appearances in the Bible (14 section 41), as he later does with the word *nasa* (15 section 4). The same attention to philological matters is evident in his comments on the etymology of the Greek terms for "fate" and "destiny" (13 sections 14, 16) and in his correction of the Vulgate translation of Wisdom 8:1 (13 section 7).

For all their density of thought and expression, the *loci* are also generously leavened by homely illustrations which serve to clarify the often labyrinthine paths of Vermigli's arguments, or to support them through arguments from analogy. Chief among these is the image of God as an artisan or craftsman, a metaphor that goes back to Plato's *Timaeus* (13 sections 6, 8; 14 section 1). One memorable iteration of this analogy evokes the workshop of a blacksmith, equipped with tools of differing character, whose uses may not be readily apparent (13 section 9). Elsewhere, God's method of turning evil things to good ends is sym-

---

38. Amos, "Exegesis and Theological Method," 192.

39. On this subject see Max Engammare, "Humanism, Hebraism and Scriptural Hermeneutics," in Torrance et al., *Companion to Peter Martyr Vermigli*, 161–74.

bolized by the purposive use of poisons by the doctor or magistrate (14 section 9), the beneficent function of ulcers (14 section 25), or the way princes employ the ferocity of wild beasts to punish their enemies (14 section 40). Again, the relationship between *habitus* and privation is illustrated by that of sun to darkness (14 sections 7, 33). In a simile adapted from Thomas Aquinas, the relationship of *per se* and accidental causes is imaged by a master who sends two servants to the same location without telling either of the other's presence (13 section 4). Such illustrations exemplify Vermigli's humanist concern with rhetorical artistry and persuasive appeal.

About the Translation and Sources

The Latin text which forms the basis for this translation is the first edition of Vermigli's *Loci Communes*, edited by the French pastor Robert Masson and printed at London by John Kyngston in 1576 under the title *Petri Martyris Vermilii Florentini praestantissimi nostra aetate theologi Loci Communes*. The only complete English translation of the *Loci* comes from the hand of Anthony Marten; it was published in London in 1583 by H. Denham and H. Middleton as *The common places of the most famous and renowned divine Doctor Peter Martyr divided into foure principall parts: with a large addition of manie theologicall and necessarie discourses, some never extant before*. The entirety of *locus* 13 and the first 37 paragraphs of *locus* 14 have been previously translated by Joseph McLelland as part of the miscellany volume *Philosophical Works* in the Peter

Martyr Library.[40] Readers seeking more information about the Aristotelian and scholastic sources behind Vermigli's argumentation in these pages will find helpful guidance in McLelland's notes, although he misses or misattributes a number of quotations from classical poets and patristic authors.

The sections translated here contain occasional textual discrepancies, some of which are catalogued in the footnotes. In quarrying variant readings, I consulted two later editions of the *Loci Communes*: the first Zurich edition of 1580 and the first Heidelberg edition of 1603. I also referred frequently to the first editions of the three commentaries in which these three *loci* originally appeared. In the footnotes, these commentary editions are identified by Bible book and date of publication: thus, Genesis 1569, Samuel 1564, and Kings 1566. I did not prepare a full collation of the London 1576 edition against the commentaries; thus, textual divergences are noted only when they affect the textual tradition of the *Loci Communes* themselves. Furthermore, not all discrepancies are marked in the notes: I have omitted many trivial errors in the later editions, as well as corrections made to the attribution of biblical passages (especially the numbering of Psalms). In most cases of disagreement, the correct reading is fairly plain; only in a few vexed spots did the divergence between editions seem to warrant editorial comment. In several places, the reading of the London 1576 edition is

---

40. Joseph McLelland, ed. and trans., *Philosophical Works: On the Relation of Philosophy to Theology* (Kirksville, MO: Truman State University Press, 1996), 176–96 and 215–62.

clearly mistaken, and there my translation restores the correct text as transmitted by the original commentary.

Vermigli's Latin is dense and unwieldy. In crafting this translation, I have aimed to balance fidelity to the grammar of the text, and especially to the author's technical terminology, with a readable and readily comprehensible English style. Accordingly, I have frequently broken up Vermigli's long sentences into shorter units, and have added paragraph divisions within the sections (all of which are unbroken in the Latin editions). As a further aid to the reader, chapter headings have been created within each of the three *loci* to help the reader synoptically grasp of the flow of Vermigli's argument. I have striven to maintain the greatest feasible consistency in the translation of key terms, although some, such as *ratio*, defy uniform renderings. While the final product is grounded in a close study of the original Latin text and punctuation, I have consulted Marten's relatively literal and faithful (albeit, to modern ears, archaic-sounding) vernacular translation of the *Loci* at many points, and on occasion I have adopted his renderings, although my interpretation of the Latin text differs from his at a number of points. I consulted McLelland's translation only after completing my own. McLelland frequently omits conjunctions, reorders clauses, prunes wordy phrases, simplifies tenses, and, in particular, translates key Latin terms (like *obligatio*, "liability"; *velle*, "to will"; and *privatio*, "privation") in many different ways. Partly for these reasons, although his translation is highly readable, it not infrequently masks the flow of Vermigli's thought and introduces many errors. In comparison with McLelland's translation, I have tried to preserve more of the uneven character and occasional turgidity of Vermigli's prose, including his frequent use of the vivid present tense and his penchant to sometimes heap up short, staccato clauses in a paratactic sequence.

Peter Martyr's exposition is suffused with citations of Scripture. All direct quotations have been identified using in-text citations. Vermigli's text of biblical passages often differs from the Latin Vulgate. Sometimes the alternative wording is due to his penchant for quoting Scripture from memory; at other times it is occasioned by the broader context in which the quotation appears, or deliberately chosen on the basis of his familiarity with the Greek or Hebrew original. I have rendered these Scriptural citations in accord with Martyr's *ipsissima verba*, without resorting to any particular biblical translation.

The same applies to my translations of Vermigli's frequent citations of the Church Fathers and of medieval philosophers and theologians. The sources of all such citations are catalogued in the footnotes. Where standard English translations exist, such as Philip Schaff's *Nicene and Post-Nicene Fathers*, the reader will find a reference to a published translation alongside a locator in the Latin or Greek text. In other cases, references are made to J. P. Migne's editions of the *Patrologia Graeca* and the *Patrologia Latina* (*PG* and *PL*, respectively). Full identifying information for the translations of original sources—and for the Latin and Greek editions, excepting individual volumes of *PG* and *PL*—can be found in the bibliography under "Primary Sources."

Other footnotes explain the meaning of important technical terms and their usage by previous authors, or explain allusions to key topics of debate in ancient and medieval disputations about providence and the cause of sin.

The material for the thirteenth *locus*, entitled "On the Providence of God," is drawn from two of Vermigli's commentaries:

> sections 1 to 4:
> *In primum librum Mosis, qui vulgo Genesis dicitur commentarii doctissimi*. Zurich: [C. Froschauer], 1569. Digression on "Providence" at Genesis 28:16 (115^v–116^v).

> sections 5 to 16:
> *In duos libros Samuelis commentarii*. Zurich: [C. Froschauer], 1564. Digression "On the Providence of God" at 1 Samuel 10:2 (56^r–59^r).

The material for *locus* 14, "Whether God is the author of sin," is drawn from the following:

> sections 1 to 37:
> *In duos libros Samuelis commentarii*. Zurich: [C. Froschauer], 1564. Digression "Whether God is the author of sin" at 2 Samuel 16:22 (275^r–285^r).

> sections 38 to 42:
> *In duos libros Samuelis commentarii*. Zurich: [C. Froschauer], 1564. Digression "Whether God is the author of sin" at 1 Samuel 2:24 (20^v–22^r).

> sections 43 to 44:
> *Melachim, id est, Regum libri duo posteriores*. Zurich: [C. Froschauer], 1566. From Vermigli's comments on 1 Kings 8:14–21 (62^r–62^v).

Finally, *locus* 15, "In what sense God is said to repent and to tempt," is drawn from:

> sections 1 to 3 (down to *id ipsorum vitio fieri*):
> *In duos libros Samuelis commentarii.* Zurich: [C. Froschauer], 1564. Digression "In what sense God is said to repent" at 1 Samuel 15:15 (85^v–86^v).

> section 3 (from *Sed antequam alterum caput*) to 7:
> *In primum librum Mosis, qui vulgo Genesis dicitur commentarii doctissimi.* Zurich: [C. Froschauer], 1569. Digression on "Temptation" at the end of Genesis 22 (90^r–90^v).

PETER MARTYR VERMIGLI: FIRST PART OF THE COMMON PLACES

THIRTEENTH CHAPTER
On the providence of God

[CHAPTER 1: PROVIDENCE IS DEFINED]

1. The Greeks call providence πρόνοια or προνοή [foreknowledge]. The Hebrews derive [the word *hashgachah*, "superintendence"][1] from the verb *hisgiah* in the Hiphil, meaning "to precisely see and distinguish." As for its definition, Cicero says in his book *On Invention*, "It is that by which something future is foreseen before it takes place."[2] But if this definition be applied to divine providence, it does not capture the latter, because that definition denotes merely knowledge of the future and the faculty of knowing in advance, whereas divine providence includes not only the knowledge of God's mind but also his will and

---

1. Here the original version, Genesis 1569, inserts the Hebrew word השגחה (*hashgachah*) and lacks *deducunt* ("derive"). London 1576 and Zurich 1580 both omit the Hebrew term, while Heidelberg 1603 restores it (transliterated as *Haschgachah*). *Hashgachah* is a key notion in the rabbinic tradition and classical Jewish philosophy; that Vermigli is conversant with the term evinces his familiarity with rabbinic literature.

2. Cicero, *De inventione* 2.53.160.

choice by which it is fixed and determined that events will happen in one way rather than another. Besides these things, providence also includes the power and capacity to direct and govern the things for which he is said to make provision, since we find in things not only their very substance and nature but also the order by which they are connected to one other and tend one to another, such that one thing helps another or one thing is completed by another. And things have been well ordained in both of these respects, for all of them were said to be good individually with regard to themselves and to be very good generally with regard to order. That this order exists in things can be proved from the very nature of order. For Augustine defines *order* as an arrangement of equal and unequal things that allocates to each what belongs to each.[3] And everyone knows that the parts of the world are varied and unequal if they be compared with one another. Further, both the testimony of experience and the teaching of the sacred writings show how fittingly God has allotted to every one of them their own places and their proper spots and positions. For we are told that God set a limit for the sea and the waters and that they do not dare to go beyond the boundaries prescribed for them [Prov. 8:29], and further that he measures the air with the hollow of his hand [Isa. 40:12], and so on.

Since so great a benefit received from his hand is to be ascribed to him by reason of providence, we will be able to define it: *providence* is the system[4] which God uses

---

3. Augustine, *De civitate dei* 19.13.1 (*City of God*, NPNF 1/2:409).

4. The Latin term Vermigli uses here is *ratio*, which has a wide range

in directing things toward their proper ends. This definition includes not only knowledge but also the will and the power to accomplish the thing. Accordingly, Paul brilliantly expressed what we are saying in the first chapter of his letter to the Ephesians when he said, "Who works all things according to the counsel of his own will" [v. 11]. And in his speech *For Milo*, Cicero taught by what indications this providence can be grasped from natural reason. For he writes, "No one can judge otherwise except a person who thinks that there is no heavenly power or divine sway, and who is not moved either by the sun out there or by the movement of the skies and heavenly bodies or by the alterations and orders in events," and what follows.[5] Paul described this same proof in the first chapter of his letter to the Romans [vv. 19–20], as did Job, chapter 12 [vv. 7–8]: "Ask the cattle and the birds of the sky, the fish of the sea, and the bushes of the earth, and they themselves will teach you." Likewise Psalm 19 [v. 1]: "The heavens tell forth the glory of God." And again, Job chapter 31, about the goats, deer, the horse, Leviathan, and Behemoth [Job 39, 40, 41].

---

of meanings including *system, method, plan, principle, relation,* and *account.*

5. Cicero, *Pro Milone* 30.83.

[CHAPTER 2: PRELIMINARY OBJECTIONS TO PROVIDENCE ARE ANSWERED]

2. Therefore, let this be settled: the order of things demonstrates that what was created was not made haphazardly or by chance; therefore, God is a purposeful agent, and all things are subject to his providence as to a certain all-embracing and supreme art, and nothing can be found that evades it. However, some have dared to deny this. They entrust only certain very high and paramount matters to God's care, while ascribing the rest—the smallest matters—to natural causes, and leaving the relatively important matters be carried out by angels or demons. One can see this in Plato's *Protagoras*, where the creation of things is described such that certain things were granted to Epimetheus to make, others to Prometheus.[1] The only thing that is claimed to have been accomplished by the work of the gods is taking thought for the best interests of the human race. But Christ teaches us otherwise in the gospel: "The hairs of your head are all numbered, and of two sparrows not even one falls without the will of your Father"

---

1. Plato, *Protagoras* 320c–322a.

[Matt. 10:29–30]. "And the Lord himself looked out from heaven upon all the children of men" [Psalm 14:2].

Now if those men were interpreting the matter to mean that there is not providence over all things in the same way that there is over human beings, we would grant this—not because providence, despite being absolutely simple in itself, ought to be called multiple, but because the effects that it directs are varied and diverse, and so providence itself also seems to have diverse ways of being. Thus we concede that the providence over upright persons is greater, to such an extent that, in comparison with them, the Lord could say to the damned and to the foolish virgins, "I do not know you" [Matt. 7:23; 25:12]; and by the same token, it concerns human beings more than it does irrational creatures.

And from living faith in this providence we derive many useful benefits: above all, consolation in adversity, since we know that those things happen not haphazardly but by the will and supervision of God our Father. Also, we are spurred on more and more each day to good works, since we realize that God is aware of and witness to our actions and that he will justly judge them in the future. Besides this, the gifts which we enjoy are more pleasing to us on account of their having been bestowed on us by a provident God. Moreover, within that providence we contemplate predestination, which brings such great consolation to upright persons that they are wonderfully strengthened by it.[2]

---

2. For the relationship between providence and predestination in Vermigli's thought, see McLelland, *Philosophical Works*, xxxii–xxxviii, which includes a comparison with the views of Calvin, Zwingli, and Bullinger.

3. Nor do we need to fear any novelty in God on account of his providence. In the case of human beings, they are devoid of knowledge when they are brought forth into the light by their parents and are incapable of acquiring knowledge without change. But we should by no means surmise this of God, since he has possessed his knowledge from eternity. Besides that, he has this knowledge from his own self whereas we derive our knowledge from things. So James correctly wrote that with him there is no change or shadow of alteration [James 1:17], and it never happens that God's knowledge is changed by a change in things. Moreover, this highest knowledge is safely stationed in God: there is no looming danger that he may abuse it as do human beings, of whom it is written in Jeremiah 4 [v. 22], "They are wise only to commit evil." But God is the best and has knowledge of what is best, and anyone who has such knowledge cannot use other things evilly, as Plato taught in *Second Alcibiades*. There it is proved that in the absence of this knowledge it is better to be unaware of many things; for Orestes' interests would have been better served if he had not recognized the woman approaching him as his mother after he had resolved to kill her.[3]

This supervision of things does not mean that God is wrenched from his tranquil felicity or from contemplation of better[4] things. Such is the lot of human beings: sometimes the handling of superfluous matters distracts them from better and serious pursuits. Hence it is not without

---

3. Plato, *Alcibiades 2* 144b–c (generally considered an apocryphal work).

4. *meliorum* Genesis 1569, London 1576, Zurich 1580: *meliore* Heidelberg 1603.

reason that Paul condemned empty and meddlesome questions [2 Tim. 2:23]. This is a consequence of the restrictedness of our intellect, which is not able to direct its energy to many things. But since God is infinite in regard to all that is his, he can without any difficulty perceive all things that happen, that will happen, or that have ever happened.

Nor does this knowledge of things spur God to evils. That does happen to human beings, because their appetitive faculty has been corrupted. Hence Solomon said, "Do not look at wine when it gleams golden in the glass," etc. [Prov. 23:31]. Psalm 109 [119:37]: "Turn away my eyes from beholding vanity." And Job in chapter 14 said that he had made a covenant with his eyes that he would not think about a virgin [Job 31:1]. But since God is the first yardstick of justice and integrity, he cannot be impelled to evil. Yet Averroes said, "Certainly his intellect would be cheapened if he discerned and apprehended all these lower things."[5] However, because he acquires that knowledge not

---

5. Ibn Rushd (1126–1198), known to the Latin West as Averroes, was an influential Islamic philosopher and polymath. He held that the First Form "understands nothing outside itself" (*Long Commentary on the* De Anima *of Aristotle*, trans. Richard C. Taylor [New Haven: Yale University Press, 2009], 3 §5, 326), and that "if it is not possible for it to think what is lower, nor that which is better than itself—since there is nothing better than itself—then it thinks only itself" (Charles Genequand, *Ibn Rushd's Metaphysics: A Translation with Introduction of Ibn Rushd's Commentary on Aristotle's Metaphysics, Book Lām* [Leiden: Brill, 1984], §1700, 194). For Averroes, God, the Prime Intellect, does not have either a universal or a particular knowledge of the created world. Nevertheless, the First Principle is not ignorant of what it has created: it knows them in a manner unique to itself, by virtue of its being their cause. See *Averroes' Tahafut Al-Tahafut (The Incoherence of the Incoherence)*, trans. Simon Van Den Bergh (London: E. J. W. Gibb Memorial Trust, 2012), 2 vols. in 1, §468 (1:285);

from things but from his own self, this conclusion is not to be granted nor does it actually follow. Similarly, when we behold a mirror, we are not contaminated because it reflects back the images of base things, nor again is the visible sun above us contaminated when its course takes it over mire and filth.

And God does not suffer from any distress in understanding. For in this action he does not use any bodily instrument, as do human beings: for them distress does arise from understanding, because the body is thereby impaired and wearied severely. Hence Solomon not without reason called this pursuit of knowing a shattering or affliction of the spirit [Eccl. 2:11]. For knowledge sometimes produces disturbance in us, because those who understand more see more things that displease them and irritate them. That is why it is said, not without reason, "He who adds knowledge adds distress as well" [Eccl. 1:18], for we have a hard time coping with things that happen unfittingly. But God is not at all subject to those human feelings, for he has something more: he sees the outcome of things and directs them, no matter how unfitting they are, and knows that they will turn out for his glory.

---

§§226–27 (1:135), §§339–41 (1:204–5); §507 (1:310). As Averroes asserts elsewhere (in his *Epistle Dedicatory*), the denial that God knows particulars "by means of a generated knowledge" (as opposed to "eternal knowledge," which Averroes does ascribe to God) is "the ultimate in removing imperfections [from God] that it is obligatory to acknowledge." Averroes' *The Book of the Decisive Treatise Determining the Connection between the Law and Wisdom and Epistle Dedicatory*, trans. Charles E. Butterworth (Provo: Brigham Young University Press, 2001), 42. For a summary of Averroes's view, see Posti, *Medieval Theories of Divine Providence*, 61–62.

[CHAPTER 3: ON PROVIDENCE, NECESSITY, AND CONTINGENCY]

4. The objections that we have eliminated so far have not been difficult to remove from divine providence, seeing that a plain and ready way out was presenting itself in regard to them. But there remain a number of other objections more difficult to solve. The first of these is based on chance and fortune, which seem to be ousted from the nature of things if we attribute to God providence over all things. For nothing is more opposed to fortune and chance than reason. Fortune, after all, is a cause which acts from an intention[1] when something happens that is not intended or decided or resolved, contrary to expectation and when we are unaware. But we resist this argument in the following way. As far as we are concerned, God's providence does not do away with fortune and chance.

---

1. Cf. Aristotle, *Physics* 2.5.197a5–7: "So it is clear that chance [ἡ τύχη] is a cause by accident of things that are done by choice for the sake of something." Medieval Latin commentators on the *Physics* debated in what sense *fortuna* can be described as *agens a proposito* or *agens secundum propositum*. See, e.g., Aquinas's *Commentary on Aristotle's Physics* 2.8.213–16.

For what prevents its being the case that nothing comes about fortuitously with respect to God, yet many things happen haphazardly and by fortune with respect to us? A rather fitting simile can be brought forward here. Suppose a master sends his slave to the market-house to stay there until the ninth hour. If he sends some other slave of his to the market-house before that hour has elapsed, the event of those[2] two slaves running into each other will not happen haphazardly or fortuitously with respect to the master, since he anticipates this by sending them to the same place; but it will not happen intentionally on their part, since the one will have been entirely unaware about the other.[3] Therefore, many things which happen under God's foreknowledge and awareness take place by chance and fortuitously if you will refer them to a dull-witted human being and his weak intellect.

But they say: If, as we believe, all things are directed by God and happen by his counsel, where will there any longer be contingency in things? Everything comes about by necessity. And some think that this argument against divine providence is so powerful that the freedom of our choice can hardly be defended. But basically the same pattern of response can be brought to bear on this line of reasoning which we used a little earlier with respect to fortuitous things. For it is possible that if you focus on the proximate causes, the things that take place rightly are contingent and are rightly so called, since it is not at all

---

2. *illi* Genesis 1569, London 1576: *illic* Zurich 1580, Heidelberg 1603.

3. This well-known illustration is adapted from Thomas Aquinas, *Summa Theologiae* I[a] q. 116 a. 1 co.; cf. also Aristotle, *Physics* 2.4.196a4–8.

incongruous for that cause to produce that specific effect just as much as its opposite. For instance, with respect to my own will, it is just as possible for me to sit as it is for me not to sit. Therefore, if those effects be referred to that cause, they will be contingent, since it is possible for them to be otherwise; but inasmuch as they are subject to divine providence, we should not in the least deny that they are necessary. At any rate, if one admits a twofold necessity, namely absolute and hypothetical, it is possible that those things which are necessary hypothetically are contingent and not necessary if you take them as outside the hypothesis.[4]

Isaiah chapter 14 deals with the overthrow of the Babylonian kingdom. This event was contingent with respect to its own worldly causes, since there was nothing preventing it from being otherwise. And yet the prophet, wishing to show that it would undoubtedly happen, focuses on the divine purpose and says, "God has so resolved: who will be able to dissolve it? The hand of the Lord has now been stretched out, and who will be able to draw it back?" [v. 27]. Thus, at this point the matter was necessary on that account. And in Psalm 37 [33:11] we read, "But the counsel of the Lord remains forever, and the counsels of his heart to all generations."

---

4. Here and in section 13 below, where these concepts are developed more fully, Vermigli uses the technical expression *necessitas ex hypothesi*, referring to "a necessity that arises out of a set of circumstances or out of a disposition or capacity hypothetically rather than absolutely or necessarily conceived." Muller, *Dictionary of Latin and Greek Theological Terms*, s.v. "necessitatis consequentiae." See also note 3 on p.35 below.

Still they push back: "Necessity seems to block divine providence. For we do not consult about things that cannot be otherwise. Therefore, since many things in the world that fall into this category are necessary, they seem to exclude divine providence." But at this point we must observe that even if all things are necessary inasmuch as they are referred to God's decree and plan as something accomplished and decided, still all things are contingent in respect to God who decides and determines the act, and therefore nothing in the world is necessary to the point that it could not be otherwise. (We are not talking now about the definitions of things or about necessary propositions or interconnections: those things are not guided by divine providence, for they are expressions of eternal truth and of the divine nature.) One also finds some people who think that there would be no evil things to be found in the world if it were guided by God's providence, since no one who acts providently in his own works would leave any place for evil. But there is an easy response to such people: no evil can be found that is not useful for the saints and that does not contribute to their salvation or manifest God's justice and mercy or promote the order of the universe or its preservation.[5]

5. In order that we may follow some method,[6] we must ask firstly whether there is any providence; secondly, what it is; thirdly, whether all things are subject to it;

---

5. Heidelberg 1603 adds a note here: "The same topic, but clearer, from 1 Samuel 10 verse 2."

6. *Vt methodum aliquam sequamur* London 1576, Zurich 1580: *Vt autem methodus intelligatur* Samuel 1564: *Verum ad haec fusius explicanda ut methodum aliquam sequamur* Heidelberg 1603.

fourthly, whether it is unable to change; finally, whether it allows for any contingency in things. But before I come to the topic itself, something must be said about the meaning of the terms themselves. *Contingent* is the term for what the Greeks call ἐνδεχόμενον [possible], referring to something of such a kind that it is able both to happen and not to happen, and whether it happens or does not happen, nothing is entailed that is absurd or contrary to reason or contrary to the word of God. It is divided into three categories. The first of these is called by the Greeks ὁποτερ' ἔτυχεν [whichever happens to be the case], referring to that which has an equal propensity in each of two directions; the second ὡς ἐπὶ τὸ πολύ [for the most part], referring to that which tends in most instances to happen in one way or the other, but is able to turn out differently; the third is called ὡς ἐλάχιστον [extremely infrequent], referring to that which happens only rarely and unusually.[7]

The philosophers lay down a twofold foundation of contingency: matter, which as it encounters in turn different acting causes takes on different forms in turn; and will, by which our actions are governed. Will has the principle of matter because it is guided and impelled by the intellect. Augustine in *Eighty-Three Questions*, question 31, says that the philosophers divide prudence into three parts: intelligence, memory, and providence, and that they refer memory to past things and intelligence to present things, while the provident man is one who can determine on the basis of past and present things what will happen later

---

7. This Greek terminology largely derives from Aristotle's *De interpretatione* 9.19a10–23 (*On Interpretation*, 139).

on.[8] Now God not only recognizes and sees what is going to take place, but also adds will to these things. For we do not postulate in God only bare intelligence, but also efficacious will by which he guides and controls all things. The Greeks call this πρόνοια [foreknowledge], and Cicero in *On the Nature of the Gods* calls it "the prophetic old woman of the Stoics."[9] She was considered of such great worth among the ancients that she was even worshipped as a goddess in Delos because she had helped Latona in childbirth. But this story indicates nothing other than that second causes, despite having some power in themselves, still do not bring anything to pass unless the providence of God supervenes. For Latona is nature; providence is a midwife: if the latter does not supervene and help and, so to speak, perform her midwifely duty, then the former does not bring forth anything.

---

8. Augustine, *De diversis quaestionibus octoginta tribus* 31.1 (*Eighty-Three Different Questions*, 58).

9. Cicero, *De natura deorum* 1.8.18.

[CHAPTER 4: PROVIDENCE EXISTS AND INVOLVES POWER AS WELL AS KNOWLEDGE]

6. But now, as concerns those five headings which I have resolved to discuss one by one from the beginning, I propose for myself in the first place the thesis that providence exists. This can be demonstrated by many extremely firm arguments. In the first place, since God is the author and creator of all things, and since he can do nothing haphazardly, but has his own fixed and determinate reasons within himself, it is necessary that providence exist. After all, since there is no artisan who does not perceive both the reasons and the ends of his own work and grasp the means by which he can conduct it to its proper ends, it would be madness not to attribute this capacity to the supreme artisan, God, whom the divine Scriptures make out to be not only the creator of all things but also, figuratively speaking, the potter. Chrysostom, in his nineteenth homily on the letter to the Ephesians, says, "If a ship, however stable and well outfitted it be, cannot hold together on the waves without a helmsman, how much less can the whole world stand firm without God's care

and direction?"[1] Again, if an architect will not start the building process before he has all the parts, shapes, and forms of the building sketched out in his mind, shall we suppose that God created the totality of all things haphazardly, without a plan, without reason? Certainly the heavenly bodies, the stars, the upper and lower air, water, heat, cold, so many alternations and changes in things that are contrary to and at strife with one another—all these would collapse if they were not upheld by some ruler. Without care and providence, our body could not be protected from inclement weather. We apply the term *provident* to people who are so strong in mind and ability that they keep all their bodily members in submission; and God holds that place in the world which the mind occupies in a human being. Besides this, the sacred Scriptures ascribe to God the overthrowing of kingdoms and prophecies and miracles which far surpass all power of nature, and finally the judgment in which God will one day render to each one according to his works. Therefore, being moved by all of these arguments and many others, we conclude that providence exists.

For we dismiss the Epicureans, whose views are expressed in this saying: "Of course this is a toil for the gods; this anxiety troubles their serenity,"[2] as well as this one: "God walks upon the hinges of heaven and does not take thought for human affairs" [Job 22:14]. The Epicureans came up with these abominable ideas partly because,

---

1. John Chrysostom, *Homiliae in epistolam ad Ephesios* 19.3 (*Homilies on Ephesians*, NPNF 1/13:140).

2. Virgil, *Aeneid* 4.379–80 (Dido speaking ironically to Aeneas).

being dull in mind, they were unable to perceive higher things, and partly because, as they were leading shameful and profligate lives, they wanted to devise this consolation for themselves to keep them from being unceasingly tormented by fear of punishment. For anyone who leads a wicked life shies away from the light; and when boys have done something naughty, they do not want their father to be in the house or their teacher in the school. As far as the first part of the topic goes, this much ought to suffice for those who are Christians: they have been persuaded of providence's existence by the word of God alone, apart from reason.

7. As for what providence is, we will easily grasp this from its definition. For it is a power or faculty of God by which he directs all things and conducts them to their proper ends. In this definition, the genus is power or faculty. God is of course perfectly simple. Nevertheless, conformably to our own capacity, we posit a twofold faculty in him, one of understanding and one of willing. God does indeed understand and see all things; but not only that: he also wills all things. Now we will not enter here into a superfluous discussion of whether in God the will is prior to the intellect or, conversely, the intellect to the will. If anyone should wish to know this, I refer him to Scotus and Thomas.[3] That power and faculty of which I

---

3. Thomas Aquinas (1225–1274), Italian Dominican friar, and John Duns Scotus (1265/66–1308), Franciscan friar, were two of the most influential scholastic theologians of the High Middle Ages. Aquinas held that the will, the appetitive power which controls human agency, is subordinate to the practical judgments of the intellect, which presents objects or acts to the will. In his view, "the intellect moves the will" as "the end moves the agent" (*Summa Theologiae* I q. 82 a. 4 co.).

am speaking pertains to quality, for it is a natural potency. The differentia is that by that power God directs absolutely all things that either are or will be. However, this is not enough: he also conducts them to their proper ends. But to which ends? To the suitable ones. And the suitable ones are those that are appointed by his counsel. Power and faculty is the cause; the effect is that things are conducted to their proper ends. At this point, we have included all the types of causes that can be assigned in this matter.[4] I say this because no efficient cause of God's providence can be ascribed.[5] The formal cause is the power of God; the matter to which it pertains is absolutely all things that exist, for we do not exempt anything from it at all. But the final cause is that all things may attain their proper ends and result in the glory of God.

From this definition we see that God's providence is not only bare[6] cognition but also a certain efficacy. For, as Paul says, "In him we live and move and exist" [Acts

---

Scotus, in contrast, argued that the "free will" (*libera voluntas*), a faculty which he distinguished from the "natural will" (*naturalis voluntas*), is self-determining and has a higher status than the intellect (see esp. *Ordinatio* III, distinction 17).

4. Vermigli is operating here within the scholastic framework inherited from Aristotle, according to which things have four types of causes: formal, material, efficient, and final.

5. The same claim is made by Vermigli's Reformed contemporary, Franciscus Junius, in his treatise *De providentia Dei*, thesis 2, in *Francisci Iunii opuscula theologica selecta*, ed. Abraham Kuyper (Amsterdam: Fred. Muller, 1882), 1:158.

6. *non tantum nudam esse* Samuel 1564, London 1576: *non tantum nudam non esse* Zurich 1580, Heidelberg 1603.

17:28]. And again, "All things are from him and in him and through him" [Rom. 11:36]. And as Solomon says, "It is man's part to prepare the heart, but God's to control the tongue" [Prov. 16:1], for we cannot move even the tongue, the most trifling part of our body, without God's providence. And Christ says, "Not even a sparrow falls to the earth without the will of our Father, and all the hairs of your head are numbered" [Matt. 10:29–30].

Some people idly fancy that God did create all things, but abandoned them afterward once they had been created. For in the same way carpenters think it enough to have finished building a house; afterward they abandon it. However, if this were the way God operated, our world would readily collapse. For a house becomes weak and collapses if it is not restored and propped up from time to time. If the mind were to leave the body, what is left to happen except that the body would become corrupted and decay?

We should not give a hearing, either, to those who say that God does guide all things, but that such guidance merely consists in his supplying a common influence to all things, which individual things draw to themselves. For this is to make God the ruler and controller of the world in name only, not in reality. If each thing, according to its innate ability, were to adapt and accommodate to itself that common influence supplied by God, then God would follow the nature of created things, whereas on the contrary all created things ought rather to follow God. But they say that just as a person who hurls a rock or discharges an arrow thinks it enough to have set them in motion at the beginning, even though he himself does not follow them afterward once they have been dispatched, so it was enough for God to have imparted a certain power to all things even though he does not continuously govern them. However, those analogies are not similar. For the arrow and the rock fall immediately, since that force in created things cannot be long-lasting. Therefore, if God did follow up that impulse of his with eternal care and providence, the whole nature of things would not hold together.

The Peripatetics, when they saw that all things in these lower regions are constantly being disturbed, stationed the providence of God above the moon, as though it would not be right for providence to concern itself about matters in these lower regions except insofar as it supplied some common influence to all things. But this is plain silliness. For the divine writings teach that those things which to us seem preeminently fortuitous are nonetheless guided by God's providence. In Deuteronomy, God says, "If an ax flying by chance out of a woodcutter's hand should strike and kill a passerby, I myself have given him into the hand of the killer" [19:5–6]. And Job chapter 14 [v. 5]: "You have established his bounds, beyond which he will not be able to pass." And the book of Wisdom—a book which, although it is not in the canon, still contains a great deal of good and pious material—has the following in chapter 8 [v. 1]: "She reaches from end to end εὔρωστος, and arranges all things χρηστῶς." "Reaches," he says, "εὔρωστος," that is, *strong* and *robust*, since "she arranges *usefully*"—for that is the meaning of χρηστῶς: not *sweetly*, as the old translation had it.[7] And even if this

---

7. The reference is to Jerome's Vulgate, which rendered χρηστῶς with the Latin *suaviter*.

usefulness is often unseen by us, still it is always of such a nature that it contributes to the glory of God.

[CHAPTER 5: NOTHING IS EXEMPT FROM PROVIDENCE]

8. But whether all things are subject to God's providence is a matter of controversy. For some affirm it, others deny it. But as we said before, if God created all things, it is certain that nothing should be subtracted from his providence. For if anything were to be subtracted from his providence, it would also be subtracted from creation. In the letter to the Hebrews it is written, "He supports all things by the word of his power" [1:3]. This is a Hebraism, for he used the expression *word of power* to mean *powerful word*. This passage agrees with the one that we quoted from Wisdom. Ezekiel calls God "the Lord of all flesh" [Jer. 32:27]. And in the book of Numbers, Moses calls God "the Lord of spirits" [16:22]. And Paul in the letter to the Ephesians: "He who works all things according to the decree of his will" [1:11]. Even Hesiod, a pagan poet, says, "It is not possible to escape the mind of Zeus in any way" [οὐκ ἔστι πῃ Διὸς νοὸν ἐξαλέεσθαι].[1]

---

1. Hesiod, *Works and Days* 105; Vermigli quotes the verse in Greek.

Still, there are those who wish to subtract human beings and free choice from God's providence, along with things that are either necessary or fortuitous. Cicero says in *On Fate* that the most ancient philosophers, like Empedocles and Heraclitus, subjected everything to necessity, whereas the Peripatetics postulated many contingent things.[2] He also says that Chrysippus, like an unofficial umpire, despite teaching that that all other things are necessary, held that human will is free as far as the first selection is concerned.[3] That is why Eusebius quips in *Preparation for the Gospel* that Democritus made men slaves, but Chrysippus only made them half-slaves.[4] Likewise Cicero in his second book *On Divination* would exclude all providence rather than have human beings to not be free.[5] Augustine ridicules this in book 5 of *On the City of God*, the tenth chapter: he says that Cicero, with the intention of making men free, made them sacrilegious.[6] Thus we see that there are those who do not think that all things are subject to providence.

But the fact that they explicitly exempt man, who is the most outstanding of God's works, seems extremely insulting to God. For it is rather the case that all craftsmen lightly esteem their paltriest works and the ones with

---

2. Cicero, *De fato* 17.39.

3. Cicero, *De fato* 17.39, 19.43.

4. Eusebius, *Praeparatio evangelica* 6.7 (*Preparation for the Gospel*, 275).

5. Cicero, *De divinatione* 2.7.18–19, 2.21.48–2.26.54.

6. Augustine, *De civitate dei* 5.9.2 (*City of God*, *NPNF* 1/2:91).

meagre value, whereas they meticulously attend to and embellish their outstanding works. Who would think that God could have lightly esteemed that work which he held to be the most precious of them all? And if this were so, what condition would we be in? What refuge would we have in the midst of adversity? David says, "Cast your care upon God and he will nurture you" [Psalm 55:22]. And Peter says, "He cares about you" [1 Pet. 5:7]. And Zechariah: "He who touches you will touch the apple of my eye" [Zech. 2:8]. And God says, "I am your shield and your wall of bronze" [Psalm 91:4]. And David says, "The Lord is my helper, and I do not care what man may do against me. If armies in camp should stand against me, my heart will not fear" [Heb. 13:6; Psalm 27:3].

9. But you will say: Many things in the affairs of this lower world take place either by no order or by a perverted one. For we see the upright being crushed and the wicked flourishing. Let us grant this is so. But does the fact that we do not see the causes of providence mean that providence does not exist? Suppose you happened to be in a blacksmith's workshop and you saw many tools, some hooked, others curved, others incised, others bent. Would you immediately find fault with all of them because they did not all appear straight and smooth? I think not. On the contrary, you would admit that you did not understand their use. You should give God the same respect, so that when you see tyrannical and wicked men enjoying prosperity, you declare them to be tools of God's providence even though you do not understand what God is going to do about them. Augustine says that God is so

good that he can extract something good even from evils.[7] Again, if there were no tyrants, what courage or endurance could the martyrs possess? God wants there to be this triumph of his own goodness; he wants there to be some persons too against whom he may wield his might and power.

But you will say: Is it not enough that people be martyrs by reason of mental preparation? True, there are brilliant virtues concealed in the minds of the upright. But often this is not enough for God. He wants to bring out those virtues into act so that they can be seen. Therefore, our eyes ought to be lifted heavenward so that our thoughts are trained not on the wicked but on God. So it is that the prophets call Nebuchadnezzar, Pharaoh, and Sennacherib axes, hammers, saws, and swords in the hand of the Lord [Isa. 7:20; 10:5, 15; Jer. 51:20]. Job did not focus on the Chaldeans or the devil when all his fortunes were completely upended, but he said, "The Lord gave, the Lord has taken away" [Job 1:21]. A doctor is considered to be skilled if he can draw out to the surface unhealthy humors that are hidden away in the body. *We* would cringe at sores and scabs, yet the doctor will say that the patient is finally beginning to recover after those things have burst. In this way, God uses the drugs and fires of persecutions to bring to light those things that previously were concealed in our minds. Let the wicked do what they wish: still they can do nothing outside of God's will. Thus, in Acts Peter says about Pilate and Herod, "They came together to do what your hand and your counsel had decreed to do" [4:27–28].

10. But you will say: Some things are necessary, such that they cannot be otherwise. Do they fall under God's

---

7. Augustine, *Enchiridion* 11 (*Enchiridion*, *NPNF* 1/3:240).

providence? On the contrary, no created thing is so necessary that, if it be referred to God, it does not have the principle of contingency. For God, as we have said, reaches from end to end and arranges all things. What is more necessary than the course of the sun? And yet Joshua made the sun to stand still [Josh. 10:13]. What is more necessary than that a fire burn if it be supplied with fuel that is suitable for burning? Hence the common maxim, "If active things be fitted to passive things, a necessary action follows." And yet God brought it about that those three young men walked around in the burning furnace unharmed [Dan. 3:23–27]. What is more necessary than that shadows follow the shining of the sun? And yet God brought it about that darkness retreated from the shining sun [Isa. 38:8]. "But what man seems to have been created and left in the hand of his own counsel? You will keep them," Ecclesiasticus says, "and they will keep you" [15:14, 16]. I admit that as far as inward causes are concerned, man was so created from the beginning that nothing was necessary for him. But we do not on that account exclude the grace and providence of God. Let us hear the divine Scriptures on this topic, for Ecclesiasticus is not counted as part of the canon. Solomon says, "The king's heart is in the hand of God" [Prov. 21:1]. But God says, "I gave them precepts" [Ezek. 20:11], and he likewise says, "I will cause you to walk in my precepts," and, "I will give you a new heart and a new spirit" [Ezek. 36:26–27]. Therefore, man is not to be exempted from God's providence.

11. Much less should we exclude those things that seem to be done fortuitously. For even if we do not see the reason of second causes, God does see it. In fact, the philosophers teach that every cause which they term *ac-*

cidental should be reduced to a cause which is *per se*. For something that is accidental cannot be a cause. Likewise, Aristotle in his booklet *On Good Fortune*, after asking why some people are fortunate while others are not, replied that this happens because of a certain impulse and influence, but one such that the impelled person is not able to give an explanation for it.[8] He says this is why it happens that some people come out[9] fortunate while others do not. And he says that this outcome is fortuitous if it be referred to our will and knowledge, and yet that impulse is an essential cause.

But this does not resolve the question. For why does it happen that this fortune is granted to one person but denied to another? The astrologers intended to supply what they thought was lacking in Aristotle. Ptolemy in his book *Apotelesmata* refers this to the stars; it is through their agency, he says, that different people are moved differently at their birth, some to fortune and others to misfortune.[10]

---

8. The *Liber de bona fortuna* was a Latin compilation of two passages on good fortune taken from Aristotle's *Magna Moralia* and his *Eudemian Ethics*, both translated by William of Moerbeke. The *Liber* was compiled in the 1260s and then subsumed into the Aristotelian corpus. The passages Vermigli alludes to here are *Magna Moralia* 2.8.1207a36–b16 and *Eudemian Ethics* 8.14.1247a32–1248b7. For the influence of the *Liber de bona fortuna* on medieval theories of providence, see Posti, *Medieval Theories of Divine Providence*, 194–265.

9. *evadant* Samuel 1564, Zurich 1580, Heidelberg 1603: *evadunt* London 1576.

10. The astrological treatise by the Alexandrian scholar Claudius Ptolemy (c.90–c.168 AD), generally known as the *Tetrabiblos* ("Four Books"), bore the title *Apotelesmatika* ("Effects") in many Greek man-

Some people called this a divinity, others a constellation, others a particular fate; Socrates called it a *daimonion*.[11] But as for why it happens more to this person than that one, why at this time more than another one, no cause can be assigned besides God's providence. But this providence is that all things be referred to God's glory. Joseph said to his brothers, "It is not you who sold me into Egypt, but God sent me on ahead" [Gen. 45:7]. In this way God says that he sent Saul to Samuel, even though Saul seemed to have turned aside to him fortuitously [1 Sam. 9; 15:1]. In this way Christ said to the apostles, "A certain man will come to meet you carrying a jar of water" [Luke 22:10]. To God's provision these things were certain, even though on the other hand they could seem contingent to human eyes.

"What then?" will you say. "Are there no second causes? Does God do nothing through angels?" We do not dispense with second causes, but we make them instruments of God's providence. For the angels are ministering spirits, and David says, "Those who do his will" [Psalm 103:21]. But although God sends angels, still he is present himself and is in charge of all things. "If I ascend into heaven," David says, "you are there; if I descend to hell, you are present" [Psalm 139:8]. For he does not issue orders to the angels in such a way that he is absent himself, as the poets imagine with Apollo. For they relate that he seated

---

uscripts. For the benign and malign influence of the heavenly bodies on human beings at their birth, see *Tetrabiblos* 1.2–3 and *passim*.

11. Plato, *Apology* 31c–d, 40a–c. In his defense-speech before an Athenian jury, Socrates described the personal divinity that inspired him throughout his life, which he called his δαιμόνιον.

Phaethon in his own chariot, and consequently the whole sky was destroyed by fire while he was away.[12] But someone will say: Sins do not depend on providence. Later on we will state in what sense sins are guided by God.[13] The cause of sin is indeed from us; but at what time and upon whom that sin must break forth, these things are in the power of God. Nebuchadnezzar was by all means going to oppress someone, but God saw to it that he oppressed the Jews rather than others.

---

12. The story of Phaethon's disastrous ride in the chariot of the Sun was retailed in Euripides' *Phaethon*, a play that survives only in fragments. Ovid tells a version of this myth in *Metamorphoses* 2.1–328.

13. See p.77 below.

[CHAPTER 6: PROVIDENCE IS IMMUTABLE AND DOES NOT PRECLUDE CONTINGENCY]

12. The next question is whether that providence is immutable. Why should it not be? For it is the yardstick of all things that are done. Malachi 3 [v. 6]: "I am the Lord and I do not change." James 1 [v. 17]: "With whom there is no change or shadow of alteration." And Proverbs 19 [v. 21]: "There are many thoughts in a man's heart, but the counsel of the Lord remains." Isaiah 46 [v. 10]: "I speak, and my counsel remains, and I do all that I will." For since providence is the will and knowledge of God, and since those things pertain to God's essence, it cannot change unless God himself were to change along with it. Of course second causes, since they are diverse, often hinder one another—as in the case of weather we see it generally happens that some influences are hindered by others. God's will, by contrast, cannot be hindered by any power.

But formerly he willed the Jewish ceremonies; later on he willed for them to be abrogated. How then is God's providence not mutable? I reply: In God the will is entirely the same and singular, but from eternity he foresaw what would be appropriate for different times. Augustine says to Marcellinus that a farmer sows at one time, reaps at another, fertilizes the soil at another; yet the art of husbandry is not mutable on that account.[1] He says that a certain doctor, Vindicianus, gave a sick man medicine and healed him. Many years later he relapsed into the same disease, and without consulting the doctor he took the same medicine. But when his condition worsened, he came to the doctor, told him what had happened, and began to complain about the medicine. Then Vindicianus said, "It's no surprise, since I did not assign you that medicine myself." At this point some people were amazed and conjectured that he was in the habit of applying some magical power. "Nothing of the sort," the doctor said. "He is now of a different age and has different humors than he did when I gave him that medicine of his before." But will this mean the art of medicine is not stable? In the same way, then, although God foresees all things, still he has not decreed that all things are to be done at the same time.

13. Now we will come to contingency. If God's providence is thus fixed, does it allow for any contingency? At this point I will make use of two distinctions; then I will give my response. There is one necessity that is simple, another that is hypothetical.[2] For when we say that God is a wise or a just God, we mean that this is necessary unqualifiedly and absolutely. Other things are necessary hypothetically: to quote the phrase bandied about in the

---

1. Augustine, *Epistula* 138.1.2–3 (*Letters*, 226–27).

2. See note 4 on p.13.

schools, "Whatever is, is necessary so long as it is."[3] Christ and the prophets predict that the city of Jerusalem will be overthrown; therefore, it will necessarily be overthrown—not because this necessity exists in the nature of the city, but because this was predicted by Christ and the prophets, who could not be deceived. "It is necessary that there be heresies," says Paul [1 Cor. 11:19]. And Christ: "It is necessary that stumbling blocks come" [Matt. 18:7]. For once we posit these causes, namely people's corrupted characters and the devil's hatred toward the human race, and once we also posit the goal of having the elect be tested, there is a hypothetical necessity that such things take place.

Moreover, there are two ways of viewing things. The first is as they exist in act, and from this perspective they have a principle of necessity, for they are no longer indefinite. For instance, to write or not to write is contingent; but if you are currently writing in act, it is no longer contingent but necessary. In this sense we say that knowledge coming from our senses is certain, because the objects themselves cannot be otherwise. Secondly, things can

---

3. Aristotle, *De interpretatione* 9.19a23–25 (*On Interpretation*, 139)—a treatise that was passed on to the Middle Ages through the Latin translation and commentary of Anicius Boethius (c.475–c.526). The passage in question was a fundamental source for the notion of conditional necessity (*necessitas conditionis*) in the medieval philosophical tradition. It was quoted, e.g., by Thomas Aquinas, *Expositio libri Peryermenias* 1.15 (*Aristotle, On Interpretation: Commentary*, 122), who referred to this as a "suppositional necessity" (*necessitas ex suppositione*), opposed to that which is "simple" (*simpliciter*). Vermigli makes use of this distinction when discussing predestination and justification in his Romans commentary; see Donnelly, *Calvinism and Scholasticism in Vermigli's Doctrine of Man and Grace,* 141–42, and James, *Predestination and Justification,* 69–70.

be considered insofar as they lie concealed in their own causes. And because causes are sometimes able, sometimes unable to produce effects, it follows that in them there is no necessary power of effecting. But if those things be referred to God, the principle is very different. For he calls the things that are not as though they were [Rom. 4:17]. For since he embraces all time and has neither beginning nor end, even all the things that will happen infinitely later in time are present to him. And the will of God also comes in here; for we must not posit in him a bare knowledge, but an effectual one [πρακτική]. And in this way I affirm that things themselves have a principle of necessity. Augustine in his *Literal Commentary on Genesis* book 6, chapter 15: "There are many ways in which mankind and other things could have been made by God, and those ways entailed some element of possibility and not of necessity; and this is from the will of God, whose will is the necessity of things."[4] And even though such things are necessary if referred to God, yet we should assess them on the basis of their own inward and proper causes and should call them contingent. For it is not necessary that the effect have the same quality as the efficient cause.

14. If you should ask why there are these two types of causes in the nature of things, such that some are restricted and necessary, others indefinite and contingent, no answer can be given except that God has placed those conditions on all things. God produces and defines and restricts all things, yet not in such a way as to disturb and disrupt the nature of things. Boethius in his *Topics* says

---

4. Augustine, *De Genesi ad litteram* 6.15.26 (*The Literal Meaning of Genesis*, 197).

that *Destiny* [εἱμαρμένη] is derived "from *stringing together* and withdrawing conformably" [ἀπὸ τοῦ εἴρειν καὶ χωρεῖν ἀκολουθῶς].[5] For God does indeed draw all things, but he yields, so to speak, in such a way that he does not disturb anything. Therefore, even though by their own nature things have an equal propensity to go in either direction, they are inclined by God more in the one direction. By its own nature Saul's will had not been more restricted toward going than toward staying. But when God willed to send him to Samuel, this will began to be inclined in the one direction. And so God brings his father's wishes to the attention of his intellect, and causes those wishes to impel his mind and strike it efficaciously, and causes whatever other yearnings for leisure and idleness could have kept him at home to all give way. So it happened that Saul's will complied with the providence of God. Yet in

---

5. A loose quotation of Pseudo-Aristotle, *De mundo* 401b10–11 (*On the Cosmos*, 407, 409), which discusses the identification of Zeus as the prime mover with necessity and fate (Ps.-Aristotle's derivation of εἱμαρμένη, "Destiny," from the verb εἴρω, "to string together," is mistaken). Manuscripts of *De mundo* transmit ἀκωλύτως ("without hindrance") rather than ἀκολουθῶς ("conformably"), although the German philologist Hermann Usener conjectured the latter as the correct reading in the *De mundo* passage. Boethius's quotation of the line—also ascribed to him by Claude Rangueil, *Commentariorum in libros regum…Tomus 1* (Paris: Ex Office Nivelliana, 1621), 1217—presumably came in his now-lost commentary on Aristotle's *Topics*, on which see Jonathan Barnes in Margaret T. Gibson, *Boethius, His Life, Thought, and Influence* (Oxford: Blackwell, 1981), 87n.8. For the image of the "chain" (*catena*) of fate in Boethius, see, e.g., his *In Ciceronis Topica* 5 (*PL* 64:1146), defining fate as *praecedentium causarum subsequentiumque perplexionem quamdam, et catenae more continentiam*; *Consolation of Philosophy* 2.prose.6, 3.meter.10, 4.meter.2, 5.prose.2; see also Cicero, *De divinatione* 1.125.

the meantime the nature of the thing is not violated, such that Saul's will was not equally free in both directions. From this we can see how necessary God's grace is for us. For our will, being depraved in every way, shifts all things in the worse direction. Further, there are many things that make our intellect dull and blind so that the will does not easily follow. Therefore, God brings what is good to the attention of our intellect; then he kindles faith and rouses the will so that we efficaciously will that good.

15. But you will say: Why is something said to be contingent when it has already been marked out by God in the one direction and thus has become necessary? I reply: Each thing is contingent based on its own properties and principles. But providence, which brings necessity to bear, is an external cause, and the name coming from such a cause should not be imposed on things. I am aware that there are many who hold that things which cannot be done by human powers are brought forward by God to the point where our will can either choose or reject them, and they bring God's providence to a stop at this point so that it goes no further. They say that when God foresees what each person wills to choose and what to reject, his foreknowledge does not prevent anything. But those claims do not sufficiently harmonize with the divine writings. For they teach that God does not look after things in such a way that he deserts them, but—as we have said—in such a way that he conducts them to their proper ends. And those ends are in the service of God's providence. For in this way Paul says that God has worked all things according to the intention of his own will [Eph. 1:11]. In this way God himself says in Isaiah, "I do all that I will" [Isa.

46:10]. And Christ says that not even a sparrow falls to the earth without the will of our Father [Matt. 10:29].

I am aware that Origen, Cyril, Chrysostom, and others, when pressed by very plain passages of Scripture such as "It was necessary for the Christ to suffer" [Luke 24:26] and "The Scriptures had to be fulfilled" [Acts 1:16], have interpreted them as follows: it is not that they happened because God foresaw them, but rather God foresaw them because they were bound to happen.[6] If these opinions that they voiced had to do with simple knowledge, then one could not find much fault with them. After all, it is not because I see someone writing that he writes, but it is because he writes that I see him writing. But when it comes to God, we cannot postulate bare knowledge in him: we must also add will, by which he directs and orders all things. And yet their statement will be true if we understand it to apply from the effect, or, as the phrase is, *a posteriori*. For by virtue of the fact that something has happened, we understand that it was God's plan for it to so happen. In any event, the Scriptures clearly state that it was necessary for Christ to die; it was necessary for the Scriptures to be fulfilled. And how were these things necessary? By hypothetical necessity, because God had foreseen them this way—not because this necessity existed in the nature of the thing.

---

6. For a famous statement of this view, see Origen, *Commentarii in epistulam ad Romanos* 7.8.5 (*Commentary on the Epistle to the Romans*, 90): "For even if we should conceive of foreknowledge according to the popular understanding, it will not be because God knows that an event will occur that it happens; but, because something is going to take place it is known by God before it happens." Cf. also John Chrysostom, *In Matthaeum homiliae* 59.1; Origen, *De oratione* 4.

16. But perhaps you will say that there are infinite causes in the nature of the thing itself due to the fact that I do not accept whole and complete causes; for I should have added the providence of God. I reply: I accept only inward and proper causes in the case of any thing whose effects are contingent because it was possible for them either to be produced or not to be produced by those causes. And I do not add providence, because it is an extrinsic cause. If it be added, then it is inevitable that some hypothetical necessity follows. For instance, Saul meets with men carrying goats, bread, and wine. The will of those men was unrestricted by its own nature, so that they could either give or not give him something. But God by his providence restricted this will in the one direction. They were going to Bethel in order to sacrifice; they came upon Saul wearied from the journey and half-dead from hunger; refreshing him seemed like the kindly thing to do [1 Sam. 10]. God presented those considerations to their minds and he bridled any other considerations that could have hindered this will. (Now this discussion of ours is confined solely to the wills of human beings. For in different circumstances, in the case of other things that are contingent, I am aware that there are countless methods which God is accustomed to use.)

We have another example of this phenomenon in chapter 12 of Ezekiel: Nebuchadnezzar moves into Syria, and while he is still on the journey he begins to deliberate at the fork in the road whether to lead his men against the Jews or against Rabbah the capital of the Ammonites [Ezek. 21:18–23]. He entrusts the matter to the lots; God controls them and conducts the king to Jerusalem. The nature of the thing itself was contingent, but once it had been marked out by God, it became necessary.

Joseph was sold and carried off into Egypt in such a way that, as far as the nature of the thing was concerned, it was possible for him either to perpetually serve as a slave or to eventually be freed. But God sends dreams to the baker and the cupbearer; Joseph interprets them; afterward a vision is presented to Pharaoh, and when none of his diviners is able to explain it, the cupbearer privately reminds him about Joseph. And so it happened that Joseph was released from prison [Gen. 40–41]. Therefore, as we have often stated by now, let it be laid down that all things are necessary if they be referred to God's providence, but of their own nature they are contingent.

But you will say: Shall the effects unqualifiedly be called contingent, or rather necessary? There are some who wish to call them necessary, in view of the dignity of providence. But I should rather call them contingent based on their own nature. However, I do not put up any fight, provided one understand this necessity to be merely hypothetical. The Greeks rightly called providence πεπρωμένη [Fate], derived from πεπερατῶσθαι [to be bounded], because it passes through all things; others call it Ἀδράστεια [Unescapable] because nothing can escape it.[7]

Someone will say that we are reviving the Stoics' opinions on fate. This is not true. For they defined their fate as necessity based on the interconnectedness of causes, and they concluded that this fate rules even over God himself. We, on the other hand, teach that God is in charge of all

---

7. Vermigli takes both these etymologies from Pseudo-Aristotle, *De mundo* 401b11–15 (*On the Cosmos*, 409).

things and uses them for his own glory. But if they postulate that fate is nothing else than divine providence, it is merely a question of terms, not of facts, as Augustine taught somewhere.[8]

Lastly, you will say that in this way there will be no place for plans, admonitions, or rebukes, since that which God wills will absolutely happen. This same objection was posed to Augustine, which is why he wrote his book *On Rebuke and Grace*.[9] Even though God has decreed for something to happen, he still does use means in order to bring it about. He wills to change a person's evil will: so he applies admonitions, speeches, and rebukes, for these are instruments and tools of God's providence. So far is the providence of God from excluding these things.

In this question we have laid down the roots and foundations, so to speak, of predestination; but we shall speak about it at another time, when the opportunity will present itself.[10]

---

8. Augustine, *De civitate dei* 5.9 (*City of God*, NPNF 1/2:91).

9. See Augustine, *De correptione et gratia* 4.6–6.9 (*On Rebuke and Grace*, NPNF 1/5:473–74).

10. The future occasion to which Vermigli refers here is uncertain, but may be the tract "On Free Choice" (see note 4 on p.165 below): see McLelland, *Philosophical Works*, 196n.96.

PETER MARTYR VERMIGLI: FIRST PART OF THE COMMON PLACES

FOURTEENTH CHAPTER
Whether God is the author of sin

[CHAPTER 1: ARGUMENTS THAT GOD IS NOT THE CAUSE OF SIN]

1. It remains for us now to deal with the question whether God is the author of sin. For both the curses of Shimei and the defiling of David's concubines seem at first glance to proceed from God. In the case of the curses, David himself indeed said that they had proceeded from God [2 Sam. 16:11], while in the case of the defiling of his concubines, this was declared through Nathan speaking on the part of God [2 Sam. 12:11]. Therefore, the question is rightly raised whether God can be called the cause of sins. And certainly there are numerous strong arguments on both sides. I shall review a good many of them, to which all the others can be referred.

It seems that God cannot truly and rightly be called the cause of sin. Augustine has a very beautiful maxim in his *Book of Eighty-Three Questions*: "God is not the author of any thing that causes a person to become worse."[1] But no one doubts that sin causes people to become worse;

---

1. Augustine, *De diversis quaestionibus octoginta tribus* 3 (*Eighty-Three Different Questions*, 37–38).

therefore, God cannot properly be called the author of sin. It is improper that God should wish to deform man; artisans desire to adorn their own works. Secondly, God himself testifies in the whole of Scripture that he is an avenger of sins. If he is their avenger, he is not their author, for then he would be punishing what is his own. If he were truly the cause of sin, he would be condemning what he has made, and this is absurd. Thirdly, God is said to love what he has made and to hate none of the things he has made. But he testifies that he hates sin; therefore, he does not spur anyone to commit sin. To hate and to love are opposite things; therefore, they cannot both be predicated of the same thing at one and the same time. If he harbors hatred for sin then he does not love it. But if it were made by God, he would love it: God loves all the things he has made.

If God were the cause of sin, he would sin in producing sin. If someone commits theft, he is a thief; if someone commits murder, he is a murderer. But far be it from God that he should be called a sinner or be said to sin. What is it to sin if not to depart from the appropriate end? But God is infinite; he cannot be drawn away from the end by another more powerful force. He is not ignorant, such that he could depart from the end, for he is perfectly wise. And it seems absurd that he should himself make others to sin.

Let us consider what happens among these natural things that God has created. There are many efficient causes, and we see that the aim of each efficient cause is to make the thing on which it operates similar to itself. If fire ignites logs, it makes it so that the objects upon which it acts become similar. A man generates another man. In created things, agents have this property. Why should we not say that in the things of God, his aim is to make people similar to himself? Hence, to make them not to sin.

The sacred Scriptures suggest the same thing. They introduce laws that stimulate good works, never sins. If God were to incite sins or will for them to happen, he would seem to be a hypocrite, secretly and privately doing something different than what he exhibits publicly. Jeremiah said of the false prophets, "They themselves were running and I was not sending them: they were prophesying, and I had not spoken with them" [23:21]—that is, I had not told them to say this. Hosea: "Your salvation, O Israel, is from me, but destruction is from yourself" [13:9]. And everyone knows that the cause of destruction is sin. If destruction was from Israel, then so was sin. But salvation and the things that precede it are from God. If the effects, salvation and destruction, are so distributed, the causes also must be distributed such that the one belongs to God and the other to man. Sin will be from men; the virtues, from God. This is taught more clearly in John chapter 8 [v. 44] when he is discussing the devil. He says: "When he speaks lies, he speaks from his own." If he speaks from his own, he has no need to be incited by another. And again: "This is the condemnation of men: that the light has come into the world, yet they themselves loved the darkness more" [John 3:19]. James testifies that God tempts no one [James 1:13], but through temptation people are incited to commit sin; therefore, if God were the cause of sin, he could not be said to tempt no one. It is by concupiscence that we are tempted; however, concupiscence comes not from God but from the world.

2. There is a very beautiful passage in 2 Chronicles, the last chapter [36:15–17], where the cause of Jerusalem's destruction is assigned and is referred to the sins of the people. In this way the notion that God is the author of sin is rejected, since God testifies that he willed differently. Therefore, the cause is not to be transferred to God. He sent his prophets[2] to them at early morning, he says, but they hardened their heart [Jer. 7:25–26]. Christ wept over the city of Jerusalem; he was grieving about its overthrow [Matt. 23:37]. If the effect was displeasing, the cause was much more so: he was bewailing the fact they had so sinned as to deserve utter destruction. If Christ, who was not only man but also true God, was mourning, their sins were displeasing to him; therefore, God is not the author of sin.

God cannot be posited as the cause of sin unless we thrust tyranny upon him. He would be condemning men on account of their sins because they acted wickedly even though in some sense he has persuaded them to their wicked deeds. Tyrants have a habit of enacting laws and then, by their contrivances, ensuring that their citizens do something to violate those laws, in order that they may harshly punish them.

Moreover, Scripture attributes to God the judgment of all flesh. But how will he judge the world concerning sin if he himself was the author of sin? Letter to the Romans 3 [v. 5]: "If our injustice commends the justice of God, is God unjust to inflict wrath?"—in order that it may be considered an absurd notion that our sins contrib-

---

2. *Misit Prophetas suos* Samuel 1564, London 1576: *Misi Prophetas suos* Zurich 1580: *Misi Prophetas meos* Heidelberg 1603.

ute to the glory of God. For if they do, how is it that he condemns them? If the argument is valid in that case, the conclusion follows even more forcefully in this one: if God is the cause of sin, how will he judge the world? Again, it seems that we will have to designate two wills in God—and two that are contradictory to one another. But in God there is one will. If there were multiple, they would be in conflict at the same time about the same thing, such that he would will for us not to do these deeds and at the same time incite us to them. We will ask: What is the meaning of so many solemn appeals, entreaties, and summons to upright living in the sacred writings? All of them will seem hollow. Why was Christ admonishing Judas, if he willed to be betrayed by Judas? [John 13:18, 27]. These actions seem to be done in some kind of jest. But God acts gravely and seriously in his dealings with human beings.

Again, a great absurdity would follow: the distinction between good and evil, between upright deeds and sins, would be done away with. God would be reckoned the author of both. But since he is the highest good, nothing can proceed from him except good. Anyone who detests murder, adultery, or incest would have to affirm it to be a good work. Matters would get to the point where good is called evil while evil is called good. In fact, there would be no distinction between the two. For it is on the basis of the will of God, by which he forbids and enjoins particular things, that we make judgments about good and evil; but this criterion [κριτήριον] would be done away with. Likewise, the judgments of our consciences would be done away with. In the letter to the Romans we read that we have thoughts that mutually defend and accuse one another in the judgment of the Lord [2:15]. But if that other thesis were true, we will conclude that it is not oneself but God, the author, who ought to be accused.

An excuse will be supplied[3] for wicked men; they will say: Why should I repent of this deed when God himself is the author? Repentance would be removed and a window opened for great evils. For what things will we offer thanks to God? For his having freed us from our sins? But sin was good, and it would have been just as well for us to lie helplessly in sin. We will not grieve over sins but rather rejoice, since it is a work of God. It is right for us to rejoice in God's works. If God himself were the author of sin, the result will be praise and thanksgiving, not grief. God's reputation will be greatly impaired if he be reckoned the author of sin. One could also bring forward another saying they present: that God wills all people to be saved [1 Tim. 2:4]. If he wills them to be saved, he uses good means; he does not incite them to commit sin, for sins lead down to destruction. Many other arguments could be brought forward, but we will be content with these for now.

---

3. *suppeditabitur* Samuel 1564, Zurich 1580, Heidelberg 1603: *suppeditatur* London 1576.

[CHAPTER 2: ARGUMENTS THAT GOD IS THE CAUSE OF SIN]

3. Let us consider, on the other side of the question, what are the considerations which fix God as the cause of sin. In Romans chapter 1 [vv. 24–28] it is written that God handed over idolaters, who although they knew him did not glorify[1] him as was right, to a reprobate mind and to shameful affections. If he handed them over, he incited them, moved them. In Exodus it is written that he made Pharaoh's heart stupid and hardened it so that he did not listen when Moses commanded him in God's name to let the people go [Ex. 9:12, etc.]. In Isaiah chapter 6 [vv. 9–10] it is said that he blinds the people so that they cannot see. When we pour out prayers to God, we pray for him not to lead us into temptation but to deliver us from evil [Matt. 6:13]. Why would we pray this if these outcomes did not sometimes occur? No one prays to avoid something unless it is able to happen or it is just on the point of happening or he fears that it is going to happen.

---

1. *glorificarint* Samuel 1564, London 1576, Zurich 1580: *glorificarunt* Heidelberg 1603.

They like to say that God does those things and wills them not inasmuch as they are sins but insofar as they are punishments chastising the one who has sinned. But it is difficult to hold that one and the same thing is both fault and punishment,[2] seeing that the character of punishment is different from that of fault. Fault arises from the will, but punishment is inflicted contrary to one's will. If one were to accept it voluntarily, it would no longer be punishment. To hold that a thing is voluntary yet contrary to one's will seems to be an irreconcilable position.

That which is the cause of a cause can also be called the cause of the effect. And no one doubts it is from God that we have received the will, inclinations, properties, and affections by which we are incited to sinning. If we affirm that God is the cause of those things, why do we shy away from calling him the cause of sins? A thing that removes obstacles will be called the cause of any outcome or effect that later follows. What obstructs sins the most? The grace and good Spirit of God. If these do not restrain us, we will rush into the most grievous acts of wickedness. Who can remove grace or withdraw the Spirit except God alone who has bestowed them? If he removes the obstacles, he is certainly *a* cause of sins.

Again, the person who supplies the occasion for any thing seems to be the author of it. Even if he is not the principal cause, if he gives the occasion, he will not escape being called the author. God knows the hardness of Pharaoh's heart and realizes that if he is not aided by the Spirit he will be roused to commit sin. In the same way,

---

2. *culpam esse et poenam* Samuel 1564, Zurich 1580, Heidelberg 1603: *culpam esse poenam* London 1576.

the law is said to increase sin if it is not placed before the regenerate [Rom. 5:20]. "We always strive for what is forbidden, and we desire what has been denied."[3] He orders him to let the people go. What is this, if not to place before him an occasion for him to be further hardened? We cannot deny that God supplies occasions. In fact, he does not merely give occasions: we can even adduce commands by which he orders sin. In the history of Kings we are told that Ahab was wicked and God decided to punish him in war. He willed that he be induced to this by the flattering words and deceitful exhortations of his false prophets. God is introduced as speaking with the spirits: "Who is to lead Ahab astray?" An evil spirit leapt forward and said, "I will be a lying spirit in the mouth of the false prophets" [1 Kings 22:19–22]. God approves and orders, "Go and do this;" he adds incentive: "So it will be."

Moreover, we cannot deny that sin is a kind of human action. But any action, insofar as it is in act, depends on the principle of all things. God is the first act, as the philosophers also recognized; no act is possible apart from his upholding. Therefore, sin depends on God as on an efficient cause. Sins in general are motions; motions have an order, such that the lower depends on the higher; therefore, the cause of sin, at least insofar as it is a motion, is directed to its own mover.

Augustine has a number of testimonies to this fact and confirms it also by a number of passages of Scripture. In his book *On Grace and Free Choice*, chapter 21, he says that it is beyond doubt that God operates in people's minds in order to incline their wills, either to the good,

---

3. Ovid, *Amores* 3.4.17.

according to his own mercy, or to evils, according to their merits; indeed he does this by his own judgment which is sometimes manifest, sometimes hidden, but always just. At the beginning of that chapter he says, "Who would not tremble at these awful judgments of God, by which he works what he wills even in the hearts of the wicked, rendering to each one according to his merits?" And he adds, "Indeed he works also the movements of the will in people's hearts, and through them he does what he wills to do, yet he is unable to will anything unjustly."[4] He proves this by the Scriptures. In the first book of Kings we have the history of Rehoboam, who did not listen to the advice of the elders that he deal gently with the people. But it is said that this change was from the Lord, in order that he might confirm the word of Ahijah the Shilonite [12:6–15]. Therefore, as Augustine interprets, that evil will was from the Lord.

He also brings up a second passage, from 2 Chronicles 21 [vv. 8–17]. God stirred up the Philistines and Arabians against Joram because he was practicing idolatry; God willed to punish him. Doubtless the motion of the Philistines' and Arabians' minds against Joram was evil: they were invading foreign territory and were imbued with cruelty. Yet God is said to have stirred them up. In the same history of Kings the story is told of Amaziah, who provoked the king of Israel to war. Joash himself dissuaded him, as did a prophet of the Lord. But he did not listen to the holy warnings, and this was due to his ambition. Yet this was from God, who willed for him to be betrayed

---

4. Augustine, *De gratia et libero arbitrio* 21.42–43 (*On Grace and Free Choice*, 178–80).

into the king's hands because he was following the idols of Edom [2 Chr. 25].

4. In Ezekiel chapter 14 [v. 9] we read, "If a prophet has been deceived, it is I who have led him astray, and I will stretch out my hand and strike him." He is discussing the false prophets who were continuously enticing the people. Jeremiah 4 [v. 10] says that the Lord deceived the people. In Isaiah 63 [v. 17] the prophet asks complainingly why God made the people to stray, or led them astray, such that they departed from him. Solomon in Proverbs: "Like the rushing of waters, so is the king's heart in the hand of God" [21:1]. Pharaoh of course was a king; therefore, God was inclining his heart wherever he willed. Nebuchadnezzar was a king; therefore, God was inclining his will in whatever direction he had willed. In Psalm 104 [105:25] it is said of the Egyptians, "The Lord turned their heart to hate the sons of Israel": previously they seemed to love the Israelites. 2 Thessalonians 2 [vv. 11–12]: "Because people abandoned the love of truth, God sent upon them an effective error so that they believed a lie." In Joshua 11 [vv. 19–20] it is written that none of the Canaanite nations made peace with Israel (excepting the Gibeonites) because the Lord strengthened their heart to fight against the Israelites. The end is added: in order that they might be destroyed by them. That is, he strengthened them not to seek peace but to prefer war.

Moreover, the one who wills an end seems to will the things that contribute to the end, and by the same will he wills the means that make for the end. Because a doctor wills to heal a patient, if he sees that surgical cutting or cauterization or a very bitter potion is appropriate, he wills also to use those things in service of health. When

God willed that testimony be borne by the martyrs to the truth, and that Christ die, he also willed the things that led to this end, namely the harassment of the saints, the cruelty of the kings and people; for it was through these means that that end was to be reached. In the prophets, especially Isaiah, kings are said to have been like a rod, a hammer, and an ax in the Lord's hand [Isa. 7:20; 10:5, 15; Jer. 51:20]; these similes are not applicable unless God be understood to have moved their hearts. For they are not moved unless they be urged on. And when God was angry with the people of Israel, as we will learn below,[5] he incited David's heart to number that nation head by head, which was a wicked act [2 Sam. 24:1]. It is no help if you say that in Chronicles we read that Satan incited him [1 Chr. 21:1], for Satan can do nothing except what God has permitted to him. Whether God acted through himself or through Satan, you see that by God's will David was incited to something that was not permitted.

They like to make the excuse that God permits it; he does not help it. We say that this is not enough, for an affront is still left in our minds. God still seems to will sin in some way; he knows that man cannot stand in and of himself. Suppose some blind man were walking in front of us and we saw that he was about to bump into a rock or fall into a well. We are on the scene and able to help, but we are unwilling; we allow him to keep going; and when he falls, will people not say that we are guilty of this fall in some way? You were willing for him to fall if, when you were able to stop him, you did not act. Here is a still more

---

5. *quemadmodum infra audiemus* Samuel 1564, London 1576, Zurich 1580: *om.* Heidelberg 1603.

grievous example. If a weak old man were leaning on a stick and walking along in this manner as best he could, and someone took away from him the stick on which he was leaning, even if he did not impel him to fall, would people not say he was the author of the fall in some way? God takes away his Spirit from weak men who cannot go on walking without him: does he not seem to be the cause of the lapse in some way? Therefore, it will be a weak defense they bring forward if they say that God deserts men. While wanting to excuse God, we involve him in equally grievous consequences, namely that he is no longer God, and while fleeing the smoke we fall into the fire. If some things happen outside of God's will, against his wishes—if things are adduced of which he himself is not the cause—then he is not the universal cause and he is not God.

"But he does not impel the fall." That is not a complete excuse. Suppose some head of a household is rebuked because his family is behaving very wickedly. He will excuse himself by saying, "I did not order or command them." That excuse will not be considered valid: he should not have permitted what he was able to prevent. Often the head of a household is not able to prevent wicked acts, but God's power is invincible. No wills are so evil and corrupt that he cannot make them good. Anselm, *On the Fall of the Devil*, chapter 91, says, "Why do we think it absurd that God produces individual actions through an evil will, since we know that he produces individual substances that are brought into the world through a shameful action?"[6] For instance, when a son is conceived through adultery, no one doubts that the adultery is evil, yet that boy is a

---

6. Anselm, *De casu diaboli* 20 (*PL* 158:352).

creature of God. In the Acts of the Apostles, this point seems to be established twice. In chapter 2 [v. 23] Peter says of Jesus, the Son of God, that [the Jews] themselves had taken him after he had been handed over by God's definite will and counsel, and killed him. Later, in chapter 4 [vv. 27–28], when the church is giving thanks to God, it speaks like this in its prayers: "Pilate, Herod, the Gentiles, and the people of Israel came together against your Son Jesus, to do what your hand and your counsel decreed to be done." For now I will content myself with these arguments, to which still others can be added.

[CHAPTER 3: A SOLUTION IS PROPOSED]

5. Now that the arguments on both sides have been laid out, it remains to settle the question itself. I see three opinions. The first one is abominable. It is that of the Libertines who say that God is absolutely the cause of sin, and they say this in order to affirm that all sins are to be excused and not blamed, because they are works of God. If there were any fault, they would transfer it to God. Their one aim is to free everyone from the sense of sin. If someone commits murder, they say, "He did not do it[1]—God did it." And if someone does not share this opinion, they say that he is immature, unable to approve all the works of God. What more wicked thing can be conceived? The devil could not have found a readier path to hell. Let us send them off in the way of evil, since we cannot send them the way of good: let us beseech God to remove these plagues from the Church.

The second opinion is held by certain learned men who do not shy away from that meaning which the Scrip-

---

1. London 1576 and Zurich 1580 punctuate *Ille fecit* with a question mark; I have preferred the comma of Samuel 1564 and Heidelberg 1603.

tures plainly bear at first sight. They say that God hardens and that he punishes sins with sins, and then they grant that he is the cause of sin. But they add that because those actions proceed from human wickedness itself, insofar as they are from God they have the principle of justice, and human beings are not excused because they have a propensity to these actions: they do not transfer their fault to God, who plays his own part rightly. They say: If we cannot comprehend by reason how God himself acts justly and we unjustly, we should submit to the judgment of the Scriptures.[2] There are many other things which we cannot discern by human reason but which we believe nonetheless.

The third opinion is held by those who interpret all these passages of Scripture by resorting to the words *he suffered it, he allowed it, he permitted it*, or—to use the Greek terms—εἴασε [he let it be], ἀφῆκε [he permitted it], and the like. They think that in this way all dangers are avoided.

6. But as to what my own judgment is, I will not hesitate to declare it; it will be up to you to pass judgment on it later. And in order that this issue may be more easily understood, it will be worthwhile to begin further back. I will say something about evil, the genus under which sin is contained. Evil is privation, that is, privation of a good—and not of just any good, but of one that is required for the perfection of any creature; that is, one pertaining to the completion of the thing that is deprived. For if we

---

2. London 1576 punctuates this sentence with a question mark, but the period of Samuel 1564, retained in Zurich 1580 and Heidelberg 1603, is clearly preferable.

take away sight from a rock, this will not be an evil for the rock, since this quality[3] does not belong to that nature. Since evil is privation, it cannot subsist apart from good, for it must have a subject. Since the subject is nature, it is a good. Therefore, evil cannot exist except in a good, just as blindness, the privation of sight, does not hang in the air but inheres in the eye.

The point can be demonstrated in this way by many other examples. But in order not to move away from the topic we are discussing: sin itself deprives human action of seemliness and of obedience to the word of God. These qualities should have been present in action, but when we sin, action is deprived of those goods. And since action is a species of thing, it is good because of its own substance. Therefore, evil cannot exist except in a good. Besides this, evil is not sought after for its own sake, but people sin by reason of a good. Indeed, if some attractive appearance of good did not present itself, they would not deviate from uprightness. So great, then, is the power of good that evil cannot exist except in a good and as directed to a good. Hence, wise men have rightly said that a highest good can be allowed, but a highest evil—something that robs good entirely—cannot be postulated.[4] For then it would destroy itself: it would not have a subject in which to exist, nor an attractive appearance for which it could be sought after.

---

3. The Latin term is *habitus*; it refers to a settled disposition, or capacity, "belonging to either of the faculties of soul, i.e., to mind or to will." For Vermigli, as for the scholastics, "A faculty cannot receive a datum or act in a manner for which it has no capacity." Muller, *Dictionary of Latin and Greek Theological Terms*, s.v. "habitus."

4. Aquinas, *Summa contra Gentiles* l. 3 c. 15.

Evil (as we are now treating of it) is distinguished into punishment and fault. The term fault is applied to that which we commit contrary to God's law; punishment is that which is inflicted on account of sin and which itself also entails the privation of some benefit. For instance, when God dispenses disease, disease is a privation of health and has its place in the body of a living thing. He dispenses famine and barrenness, which is a privation of fertility and is in the earth itself. These things, I repeat, pertain to punishment. But sin has its place only in the mind, whereas punishments can be in the mind and in bodies. There is a third category to be added, namely that which is punishment in such a way that it is also sin. Just as there is original sin, so there is the tinder which is left behind after baptism.

With these points now laid down, I propose for confirmation an opinion or proposition that has two parts: first, that God is not the cause of sin through himself and properly; second, that nothing happens in the world, not even sins themselves, apart from his will and choice or providence.

[CHAPTER 4: THREE TYPES OF DIVINE ACTIONS]

7. If the statement is to be proven, it has to be confirmed in both parts. Let us deal with the first one: that God is not the cause of sin through himself. The arguments that were set forth in the first place support this conclusion.[1] But I add that when good and evil are opposed to one another as quality[2] and privation, the quality never brings on the privation through itself. Light itself always illuminates; it never brings on darkness. Therefore, if we posit that good and evil are opposed as privatives, evil will not come from good. Now God is the highest good; therefore, we will posit him as a quality; therefore, he does not cause privation through himself and properly. But I have said that he is not the cause of sin through himself and properly. The reason I added these qualifiers is that if we were inclined to speak less properly, we could in some sense call him either the beginning or the cause of sin—not the proper cause, of

---

1. See sections 1 and 2 on pp.45-50 above.

2. See note 3 on p.61 above.

course, but that cause which the philosophers call *a cause that removes the obstacle*.³

I will prove the point by similes. The whole sun is bright; its proper effect is to illuminate; yet in a certain sense it can be said to create darkness—not insofar as it shines but insofar as it moves and departs from one place to another. For bodies are round; therefore, when it departs, on account of its motion it cannot always shine in that place from which it withdraws, but shadows come in between. Thus, it is said to create darkness in some sense by its departure, because the bodies are arranged in this way and the sun itself is moving. The same thing also happens with a dilapidated house. It is being held up by a column; someone comes and removes the column; the stones and structures fall from the top. They fall under their own weight, and they have the cause of collapse in themselves. However, the person who removes the column is said to cause the collapse in some sense, because he removes the prop which was preventing⁴ collapse. In the same way, God is good in his own nature, but inasmuch as he is just, he wills to punish sinners, takes away grace, and in some sense can be called the cause of those things which are evilly done afterward—but not the true cause; for this proper cause is inward: it is their evil will.

And a reason can be assigned for why he sometimes takes away his Spirit from people. He removes grace from

---

3. In Latin, *causa removens prohibens*. Thomas Aquinas uses the term in his account of accidental causality in *Summa Theologiae* I–II q. 85 a. 5, discussing God's withdrawal of original righteousness.

4. *prohibebat* Samuel 1564, London 1576, Zurich 1580: *prohibeat* Heidelberg 1603.

those sinners not only in order to punish them, but in order that the superior excellence of his favor may be recognized and that we may know that the gifts of God are given by him gratuitously and do not have their source in nature. For if we possessed them at all times and in the same way as if God did not occasionally relax his strength, we would ascribe the good things we do to our own strength. But things are this way in order that we may recognize our weakness and pray more fervently for the preservation and increase of the heavenly gift. But when God's grace and favor is justly taken away from us, sin spontaneously takes its place, nor is there need of any other efficient cause. I repeat: there is no need of another cause besides our vitiated and corrupted affections.[5] This is seen in the similes I brought forward. If the sun withdraws, darkness follows, not from any efficient cause but of its own accord. If a quality is removed, at once the privation thereof is present of its own accord. If someone injures an eye so that sight is lost, blindness follows at once, nor is it necessary to seek any agent.

When the Manichees failed to recognize this, they erred most shamefully. They were unwilling to assign the cause of evil to a good God; but they saw that there are many evils, and they judged that evils cannot exist without a true cause; therefore, they postulated two fundamental principles. And because they saw great power on both sides, in the good and in the evil, they introduced two gods, one good and the other evil. On these points there is a great deal to be read in Augustine. But the evil which

---

5. *affectibus* Samuel 1564, London 1576, Zurich 1580: *effectibus* Heidelberg 1603.

is sin arises if the Spirit of God is taken away; for it is then that a human being is left to himself. But is he left in such a way that God does nothing further about him or his sin? In order that this issue may be understood, I will unfold a threefold principle of operation which we can recognize in God concerning his creatures—not because other operations of his could not be pointed out, but because those three are most relevant for the present issue.

8. An action of God is general when by his providence he nurtures, sustains, and governs all things in their proper conditions, qualities, and inclinations, as they had from the beginning when they were created, and in this way the order of nature—a thing most beautiful to ascertain—is preserved. We see that the sky retains it own nature; it obviously has many things to be marveled at. We see the violent nature of fire, the pleasant nature of air, the permeating nature of water; also metals, trees, and the works of artisans which are clearly worthy of admiration. All these things are governed by God. In fact, if he were to withdraw his hand, they would depart into nothingness. Certainly consideration of that divine governance is extremely useful. God often in the Psalms exhorts us to magnify God on account of these works. In Romans 1 [v. 20] it is written that through these creatures the Gentiles knew God and a certain eternal power, act, and governance of his, as well as his divinity. And so, as Aratus said, "Thus we are God's offspring" [θεοῦ ὡς γένος ἐσμέν].[6] We have a very beautiful example of this work in our own persons: the

---

6. Aratus (c.315–c.240 BC) was a Greek didactic poet. Here Vermigli quotes (in Greek) the fifth line of his astrological poem *Phaenomena*, which is also quoted by Paul in Acts 17:28.

soul, which is not seen and[7] which has no parts, still sets in motion and gives life to the whole body. Thus all creatures retain their proper inclinations and properties.

9. In the second place there is another work of God by which creatures not only are preserved and guided but comply with God's plans. For God uses the actions of all things, also of men and of evil men: he uses them, I say, in order to establish his plans. When he favors his own, he gives them abundant produce of crops; the seasonable and the late rains come. But if he wills of his justice to punish wicked men, nothing succeeds: a brazen sky is given and an iron earth; if the crops are ripe, they perish in a single night. Those events are not to be ascribed to fortune. When we fail to ascertain the cause, we posit fortune. Hence the poet says, "We make you a goddess, Fortune, and we station you in the heaven."[8] Therefore, we should not occupy ourselves merely in that general consideration of the world's affairs, but should ponder the function by which they serve divine providence.

Although sin comes from its own causes, namely our depraved will and corrupted affections, still even sin itself serves God. Here is a simile. There are many poisons in the world; they have harmful and damaging qualities; but a doctor makes recourse to them and a magistrate uses them rightly. A doctor makes sick people well by tempering poisons; at Athens, a magistrate used to administer poison to criminals to kill them. In this way Socrates was forced to drink the hemlock. And so even though poisons are bad,

---

7. *et* Samuel 1564, London 1576: *om.* Zurich 1580, Heidelberg 1603.

8. Juvenal, *Satires* 10.365–66.

the magistrate and the doctor can use them well, for the well-being of the state and of the sick. In this way God directs sins, which have their own depraved causes, in order to fulfill his plans and bring them to act.

I can use another simile too. The things which seem to us to happen fortuitously in the world are fully in the service of God's providence. For the Lord says in the law, Exodus 21 [v. 13] and Deuteronomy 19 [v. 5], If two people go into the forest to fell trees, and an ax flies out of the hand of the one and the man closest to him is struck and killed by it, he did this unwittingly; he will not be guilty of death. For God handed him over, and he did this for just reasons, by a fixed plan, which we do not understand but he himself knows. Thus, those who sin are indeed carrying out their own purposes; they have decided for themselves what their intention is; but God makes use of those actions. Thus, through Shimei's cursing God wills to make David's patience plain to all and to manifest his own judgments against David's adultery and murder, but Shimei wills to display his own hatred against David [2 Sam. 16:5–13]. God accomplishes what he wills with those crimes which people have committed with a different purpose—not to[9] comply with God's will but to comply with their own depraved lusts. And to return to the piece of evidence I have already brought forward: the man who is engaged in felling trees wills this, but his ax strikes another man and the striking serves God's plan. Jerome writes on chapter 12 of Jeremiah, "Nothing good

---

9. *non ut* Samuel 1564, Zurich 1580, Heidelberg 1603: *ut* London 1576.

or bad happens haphazardly and without providence, but all things happen by God's judgment."[10]

Therefore, creatures are like instruments in the hand of God; he uses them according to the plan of his own counsel. Nevertheless, these instruments are not all in the same category. For we find that some of them do not know or feel or will, and nonetheless they serve God; but others feel and understand and will the things they do, and yet they do not always act with the intention of serving God. On the contrary, often they unwillingly or unwittingly accomplish what God wills. Therefore, we will say that animate and inanimate things, sentient and non-sentient things, the good angels and the bad, and all creatures without exception are instruments of God which he uses according to the plan of his own providence. He used the Assyrians, the Chaldeans, the Persians, the Greeks, and the Romans in order to afflict the wicked Hebrews; he also used the devil against Saul and against Job.

But we must further consider that when God uses creatures, especially rational ones and evil ones like evil men and devils, he does not use them in such a way that they themselves do nothing. They too, on their part, apply their own depravity, but God uses it. God does not deal with them as with stones which feel nothing: they will, they know, and they feel. And when depraved men and the devil act evilly and are moved by their own lust, they serve the use of God's providence. Certainly they feel and will—not because their intention is such that they will to serve God, for they are pursuing their own ends, and they

---

10. Jerome, *Commentarii in Ieremiam prophetam* 3.12.4 (*PL* 24:788).

are not moved by a higher cause such that they do not apply their own wickedness.

10. But you will say: If in this way God as the highest cause concurs in those actions, and evil men as the proximate causes carry them out, the same work will belong to God and to the devil and evil men. Indeed, we ought not to deny this conclusion. But this work proceeds from the higher, good cause in a very different way and by a different reason than it proceeds from the proximate, corrupt cause. This work is evil insofar as it is the work of the devil and of evil men. It derives wickedness from the depravity of the devil and of evil men who, since they are evil trees, cannot produce good fruits. But as God, the supreme and best cause, concurs in those actions, he brings them about rightly and with order.

Both God and the devil were willing that the city of Jerusalem be destroyed, but with a different reason: God, in order to punish stubborn men; the devil, in order to sate his own hatred toward the human race. Christ had to be handed over to the cross, and this is what happened. And it was an evil work in that it proceeded from the hatred and wickedness of the Hebrews, but the same work had goodness insofar as God by that most holy action willed what he had provided in advance for the human race. Thus, in the Acts of the Apostles [4:27–28] it is said that they did against his Son the things that his counsel and his hand decreed. Yet the things they did against Christ ought unqualifiedly to be called evil, because they take their name and nature from their proximate cause, even though God rightly used them in accord with his own providence.

The devil and God harass Job with a very different purpose. The Sabaeans too and other robbers were plundering his goods in order to satisfy their hatred [Job 1:14–15]; so also the devil. But God did it so that Job's endurance might be proven, and so that by a happy outcome he might attest his own goodwill toward the upright. Thus the works were the same, but the purposes were different. Hence, when Job says, "The Lord gave, the Lord has taken away" [Job 1:21], he praises God as the highest cause, without whose providence these things were not taking place and who by his providence was using all things for an acceptable end; but he does not praise the robbers or the devil.

David too conducted himself in this fashion. He did not commend Shimei, nor did he say that those curses were good of their own nature, but he turned himself to God's providence. The work was corrupt, but in a certain sense it can be called a work of God, because he himself was guiding it and using it. Likewise it was said in the prophet, "Cursed is he who does the work of the Lord carelessly" [Jer. 48:10]. Here he calls the affliction of the people, by which wicked men were oppressing them, a work of God. So there is no grounds for wicked men to excuse their own sins due to this use that God makes of them, for they have the cause of those sins in themselves.

And just as God's good use of these things does not excuse sinners, so conversely the wickedness of sinners does not defile the good use and providence of God, who knows how to use evil deeds in the best way. Augustine in his *Manual for Laurentius*, chapter 101, shows that it is possible that God and a man will the same thing and God acts rightly by so willing while the man sins, even if he wills the same things God does.[11] He brings forward an example. The father of an evil son is sick; God wills for him to die of this disease by a just judgment. The wicked son also wills the same thing, but in order that he may more quickly come into his inheritance and be freed from his father's authority. God wills justly, but the son wills wickedly. Augustine says that, conversely, it is possible that someone wills a thing which God does not will, and nevertheless both he and God will rightly. Suppose the father who is sick has a good son. God wills for the father to die. The son piously would not will this, for he desires his father to live. They will different things, yet both of them will well. So much hinges on the purpose of the will, for very often goodness and depravity depend on this.

But a misgiving crops up. If the same work depends on God and on a man, and derives wickedness from the depravity of the man, but has some rectitude insofar as God uses it, such that nothing evades God or God's providence, why does he complain in Zechariah 1 [v. 15], "I was angry a little with my people, yet they gave help for evil," that is, exceeded the limits? It seems that the sin they commit exceeds God's providence, such that they do more than God had decreed. We reply: We should not take it that they did any more than this thing could serve the use of providence, for nothing at all can happen outside of God's will and his decrees, which are absolutely firm. Augustine in the same *Manual for Laurentius*, chapter 102, says, "God's will is invincible."[12] How then are they said

---

11. Augustine, *Enchiridion* 101 (*Enchiridion*, NPNF 1/3:269–70).

12. Augustine, *Enchiridion* 102 (*Enchiridion*, NPNF 1/3:270).

to have exceeded? Not the limits of the eternal decree, but the just measure of victory. There are certain limits, a certain appropriateness and certain laws, which ought to be preserved by victors. They exceeded what was appropriate; but we should in no way grant that they were able[13] to do more than providence willed to use.

11. We say that the third type of God's works is that which is unique to the saints, for by it he most mercifully brings many things to pass in them. After all, he reigns, he lives, he acts in us to will and to perform [Phil. 2:13]. Otherwise we are by nature unfruitful trees; we are blind; we do not will what is good. Our judgment is corrupted; our will and choice is perverse in that scum of original sin. But God refashions[14] his elect by his Spirit. We have a nature that was given from the beginning in the likeness of God, and it belongs to this nature to will, to choose, and to do both these things and those; but the fact that we are incapable in ourselves of what is good is a consequence of corruption. And it is only from the supernatural grace of God that we rightly will and that we serve God with the beginnings of obedience. Therefore, the first type of God's works, the one that pertains to universal providence, is not relevant to the present discussion. The second and third types of work do pertain to this subject.

---

13. *potuerint* Samuel 1564, London 1576: *debuerint* Zurich 1580, Heidelberg 1603.

14. *refingit* Samuel 1564, London 1576, Zurich 1580: *refringit* Heidelberg 1603.

[CHAPTER 5: GOD IS NOT THE EFFICIENT CAUSE OF SIN]

12. Therefore, although God governs even sins and evils, still he is not properly called the efficient cause. Augustine in *On the City of God*, book 12, chapter 7, speaks beautifully about perverted will when he says, "An evil thing does not have an efficient cause but a deficient one, and if someone should wish to investigate this efficient cause, it is as if he should wish to see darkness with his eyes and to perceive silence with his ears."[1] For since these are privations, there is no need for them to have efficient causes. Yet they are things that are known to us, for the same sense has contrary things as its object. Sight can only see bright things, the ear can only hear sounds, and yet by those senses we recognize even these things, not by their use but by their privation alone. And God uses perverted will for his own ends—not because he is only able to attain what he wills through these means, but because it has pleased him

---

1. Augustine, *De civitate dei* 12.7 (*City of God*, NPNF 1/2:230). Augustine held that, since all things were created good by God, there is no evil thing that could serve as the efficient cause of sin. See discussion in the Volume Introduction.

to manifest his wisdom and power in this fashion, in order to show that he is able to do something mediately and immediately, as they term it, and that it does not matter to him whether the instruments he uses are good or evil. Therefore, we must seek a deficient cause of evil actions. And among other things we find perverted affections and inclinations. Since these fall short of God's word and of right reason, it is not surprising if things that are defective proceed from that source. Those are inward causes of sin, but they are deficient rather than efficient.

Likewise, the devil is said to be the cause of sin. For in the book of Wisdom we read, "Through the devil death entered into the world" [2:24]; therefore also sin, for death is the effect of sin. Yet the devil cannot be said to be the proper and absolute cause of our sin. The reason is that a proper and complete cause is of such a nature that once it be posited, the effect necessarily follows. But this is not the case with the devil. However much he on occasion suggests evil things to the upright, sin does not always follow, for of course many saints steadfastly resist him. And since sin does not follow, he cannot be said to be an absolute and complete cause of sin. He does incite men, but not in such a way that sin follows necessarily.

I could bring forward another argument. Let us imagine that the devil himself had not defected from God, and that man had been created. Man would still have been able to sin by his own nature, and he would have had the cause of sin in himself, but the prompting of the devil would not have been a cause of sin, since he would not yet have been estranged from God. Besides this, the devil cannot induce the will to commit sin of necessity. Therefore, he is an imperfect cause of sin; not a complete one, but an urging and attracting one. Thus we have stated from what source sin has a deficient cause, namely from our own corruption.

Yet God guides and governs sin itself. He does not look on idly; he plays the part of a judge and governor; he does not leave all things without reins. But in what sense is he said to guide sin? In regard to time, manner, type, matter, such that it is bent now against this man, now against that one. Our depravities lie hidden in ourselves, but God does not permit them to run riot at just any time, nor for as long as depraved men wish: he restrains sins, he cuts them short sometimes. Moreover, he brings it about that our depravity veers more in one direction than another. By God's providence Shimei's rage is bent more against David than against someone else, and more at this time than another one. God was directing Nebuchadnezzar's strength more against the Hebrews than against their neighbors.

[CHAPTER 6: GOD SUGGESTS THINGS THAT MEN TAKE AS OCCASIONS TO SIN]

13. There is likewise another factor to be considered with sins when they break out into act. God himself suggests some things which are good of their own nature, but because they meet with depraved men, they are taken in an evil direction and become occasions for sinning, so that sins which previously were lying hidden break out. However, those suggestions, inward or outward, cannot properly be called causes of sin, since they are inside of human beings; yet they can be called occasions. But some occasions are given and some are taken, just as they distinguish with a stumbling block. A stumbling block taken is an occasion for offense—not on the part of the giver, for he does what is useful; but the evil man interprets this evilly: it is a stumbling block taken. Thus Christ says of the scribes and Pharisees, "Permit them: they are blind and guides of the blind" [Matt. 15:14]. The apostle taught that people ought to act rightly, and if others should be offended, the blame would not attach to them [Rom. 14:1–9]. Now a stumbling block has been given when we do what we should not have done. But it is not so in God. He sug-

gests some things that are good by nature but, when they meet with an evil nature, become occasions of sinning.

14. This fact needs to be shown by examples. An upright man sees someone sin; he goes to him; he earnestly warns him to beware. The thing that is being suggested is good, but it meets with a depraved mind; he begins more and more to break out into hatred of virtues and to rage against good men. The admonition was an occasion for these things to break out into act. Through the upright man God was suggesting something that is good by nature, and so he is said to act rightly, for he acts from duty. Thus, for evil men good things become occasions of sinning—and of sinning more heinously than if perhaps these good things had not been afforded.

But there is this difference between us and God: when we suggest good things, we are unaware whether that man will thereby become worse, but God is not unaware. For example: God sends Moses and Aaron to Pharaoh; he orders him to let the people go. That suggestion is good by its own nature, but Pharaoh takes it evilly; he begins to rage even more. If this suggestion had met with an upright man, he would have said, "I ought to obey God, and because he wants me to let the people go, I will absolutely do it, for I have no right over that people except for so long as he himself wills." But when Pharaoh hears these things, he begins to blaspheme and says, "Who is that God of yours?" and he breaks out into savageness [Ex. 5:1–9].

We will illustrate the same fact by other examples and testimonies of the Scriptures. Not only is the admonition that was made to Pharaoh through Moses and Aaron a good thing, and applied by God externally, and that man, being evil, uses it evilly; but we have the same thing in the letter to the Romans, chapter 7 [vv. 8, 10, 12, 14]: "The law is holy and spiritual, but it worked concupiscence and death in me." God's command by its own nature is directed to life, but the tinder takes an occasion through the things that are suggested. And this does not only happen outwardly, but sometimes God also brings this about inwardly through good thoughts. For we must reckon that whatever things are good always have their source in God. The Pharaoh who came after the death of Joseph began to think to himself, "I must see to it that the state not suffer any harm." This thought is good; therefore, it proceeds from God. But it meets with an evil mind; therefore, it is twisted against the Hebrews. For he says, "The Hebrew people is growing and will crush us when an opportunity arises; therefore, it must be annihilated." He publishes an edict that the male children of the Hebrews are to be thrown into the river [Ex. 1:8–16]. The first thought was good, but because of his vice it veers into evil.

Nebuchadnezzar says that it is not proper for a good ruler to be at leisure; rather, he ought to put his own power to use. The thought was good, but he turns his attention toward foreign nations and does not mobilize his power against the crimes of his own people as he should have. As we read in Daniel, the same man, while he is in his palace, reflects with himself on the victories he has achieved and the greatness of the dominion he had obtained [4:29–30]. These thoughts are good, for we ought to ponder the greatness of God's benefits. But they meet with an evil mind: at once he thinks that he has established that kingdom by his own strength, and in this he sins against God.

Again, the sons of Jacob consider that Joseph is loved by his parents and is honored by God with heaven-sent dreams. That thought is good, for we ought to contemplate the works of God in others too, not only in ourselves. If they had used this thought rightly, they would have given thanks to God. But they twist it into envy; they think about taking him up and selling him [Gen. 37:1–27]. Yet God, who suggested these good things, seeing that they happen with his knowledge, does not in this case block the occasions of evils. He allows them to happen, but he is present with his own providence and governs them. Hence, through Pharaoh he wills to be glorified; through Nebuchadnezzar he wills to punish the Israelites; through the brothers who sell Joseph he wills for Joseph to be honored with great distinctions in Egypt and to provide food for Jacob's family.

Shimei sees that David is cast out and the kingdom conferred on Absalom; he says, "These are the judgments of God." That thought is good; it meets with a depraved mind; he misuses it; he insults David; he indulges his own anger and vengeance [2 Sam. 16:5–8]. Absalom got possession of the kingdom; it is suggested to him that he should listen to the counsels of the wise, that many eyes see more than one eye. A good thought, but it meets with an evil mind, and he judges that he should listen to whatever counsels are useful, even if they be wicked and shameful: he used the first, good suggestion evilly [2 Sam. 16:15–22]. God allows it; he does not will to block it; he directs it so that David's sin may be rebuked and so that God's hatred against sin may be manifested. I think that the point is now clear.

[CHAPTER 7: GOD PERMITS SIN, BUT THIS PERMISSION INVOLVES WILL]

15. But the question is raised: Since God knows that depraved men will misuse those inward and outward suggestions, good though they are, why does he suggest them? He himself has reasons for his own plans, but two reasons present themselves to us. The first is: in order his justice may be more apparent. We are blind when it comes to perceiving God's justice, but we recognize it by comparison, that is, by injustice, which we cannot see any of in God, but which we see in the devils and in corrupted men. The second reason is: in order that the recklessness of men may be restrained. For many would say: If God were suggesting good thoughts to us, we would have the will and the strength to do good things. Look: good thoughts are given, but when they meet with a corrupted nature, if it is not hindered, then because of our vice sin arises out of these things, good though they are—I mean occasions taken, but not given.

And this is how I understand what Augustine says in his book *On Grace and Free Choice*, that God sometimes inclines our wills either to good or to evil.¹ For if the things he suggests meet with good men, they are inclined to good; but if they meet with evil men, they are inclined to evil. This is also how I understand what he writes in *Against Julian*, book 5, chapter 3, that God works not only in the bodies of men but also in their minds.² This is how I also take what Zwingli of pious memory, a learned and steadfast man, once wrote: that on occasion men are incited by divine providence to commit sin, and the same evil action proceeds from God and from depraved men: justly on his side, unjustly on theirs.³ This is how I understand the passages of Scripture where God is said to hand people over to a reprobate mind or to incite them.

16. There is indeed permission there—but something more is shown by those effective turns of phrase. We too grant there is permission. For if God willed to resist, these things would not happen; therefore, he permits them. But we must know that permission is a certain type of will. It is not efficient will, to be sure, but it is a type of will. For, as Augustine says in his *Manual for Laurentius*, God permits either willingly or unwillingly. Certainly not unwillingly, because that would involve unhappiness, and there would

---

1. Augustine, *De gratia et libero arbitrio* 21.43 (*On Grace and Free Choice*, 180).

2. Augustine, *Contra Iulianum Pelagianum* 5.4.15 (*Against Julian the Pelagian*, 259).

3. Ulrich Zwingli, *Sermonis de providentia Dei anamnema* 6 ("A Sermon on the Providence of God," 181–82). Zwingli, the great theologian of the Swiss Reformation, had died in battle in 1531.

be a power greater than himself.[4] If willingly, he permits it; permission is a certain type of will.

But you ask: If he wills something in some sense, why does he prohibit it? I would ask in turn: If he does not will it at all, how does it happen? For God's will is invincible. Paul says, "Who will resist his will?" [Rom. 9:19]. God wills, and he justly wills what he wills; those who sin unjustly will what they will.

That Julian with whom Augustine disputes would have it that there is bare permission in those things, so we should understand that God does nothing at all. He said rather that God endures, and that this pertains to his patience. Augustine responds that it pertains not only to patience but also to power, because he guides sin and from it he brings about what he wills.[5] And he brings forward a passage in the letter to the Romans: "If God, willing to show his wrath and to manifest his power, has endured vessels of wrath with great clemency" [9:22]. From this indeed we see that he endures, but also that mention is made of his power. In the first letter of Peter, fourth chapter [v. 19], it is written, "Therefore, those who are afflicted according to God's will," etc. Thus he attributes the Christians' afflictions to the divine will. But they cannot suffer unless someone else acts. If he wills suffering, he wills action; suffering has its source in an agent. This will is permission, but one that also pertains to will.

---

4. Augustine, *Enchiridion* 100 (*Enchiridion*, NPNF 1/3:269).

5. Augustine, *Contra Iulianum Pelagianum* 5.3.13 (*Against Julian the Pelagian*, 254–55).

Augustine showed this in his *Manual for Laurentius*, chapter 100, while discussing that passage of the Psalm, "Great are the works of God, sought out unto all their wills" [111:2]. He follows the Greek translation; in the Hebrew we find "according to all their will." He writes: "As far as those men are concerned" (he is talking about sinners), "they have done that which God did not will. As concerns his power, they were unable to bring this about in any way. For in the very fact that they acted contrary to his will, his will concerning them came to pass; therefore, 'great are the works of God.'" He adds, "In a marvelous and ineffable way, even that which happens contrary to his will does not happen outside of his will. For it would not happen unless he allowed it; and he does not allow it unwillingly but willingly; and he, being good, would not allow evil to be done unless, being omnipotent, he could make good from that evil."[6]

God's will concurs in good things and bad things, but under different principles. It concurs in bad things indirectly: he permits them to happen; he suggests good things, but because they meet with evil men, sins ensue. But the good things he not only suggests but brings about. Yet he directs and governs even sin, so that it does not run riot against just anyone, nor at every time, nor beyond measure. Those evils lie hidden in us; but when they break out, they cannot evade God's providence. But with the good things, as I have said, he not only does not hinder them but brings them about, cooperates, and sweetly inclines our will so that we do with pleasure the things that were displeasing before. Therefore, there is one prin-

---

6. Augustine, *Enchiridion* 100 (*Enchiridion*, *NPNF* 1/3:269).

ciple of general providence, another of the use even of evil things, another of the things that he does in us after we have been regenerated.

This is how I understand the fact that Pharaoh was hardened by God and also hardened himself. For he had the cause of the hardening in himself. But God is said to have hardened him due to the suggestion and the governance; then also because in this way he directed the sin and used it for his own glory. And Paul says that God raised him up in order to display his own power [Rom. 9:17]. This is how I understand "vessels of wrath have been fitted for destruction" [Rom. 9:22]. How? Because they are prone to sinning of themselves, of their own wickedness, of their vitiated nature. Likewise, they can be said to have been fitted by God in a certain way because wickedness breaks out through the good suggestions that come from him. And when it breaks out, it is still in the hand of God, so that he may direct it this way or that, wherever he has willed. God does with a good will that which we do with a very evil mind.

Permission is a type of will, but it is not will in an unqualified sense. For, properly speaking, God's will is the cause of things. It is not like human will; we will many things which we do not bring about. Why then does God not will sin? Because sin is one of those things that have need not of an efficient cause but of a deficient one. Therefore, sin does not properly fall under the will of God. And if God be posited as not an efficient cause of sin but a deficient one, surely we shall not say that God is deficient in himself? No; but he is said to be deficient because he does not hinder, does not resist, does not assuage. What will shall this be? He wills not to hinder, he wills not to assuage, he wills not to illuminate.

17. Yet God does not force the will, either by suggesting something or by not hindering; nor is the devil capable of this. For if the will were to not act voluntarily, it would not be will, but rather unwillingness. Being forced cannot be attributed to will, any more than not being hot can be attributed to fire. Therefore, our will too is so corrupted by nature that if God's favor be taken away, it inclines voluntarily and through itself to evil. Yet it is not evil since the time it began to exist. Rather, because it was brought into being out of nothing and is strengthened and upheld by God's grace and power, if that which supports it were to be taken away, it would immediately veer to the worse of its own accord.

But if man's will is not forced to evil and is not evil from its creation, but is said to commit sin only from privation, what shall we say about the sin of the first man? In his case nature was good; grace and the help of God were not lacking; and yet he sinned. Here we say that a different judgment needs to be rendered about the first man than about our nature in the corrupted form we now have it. God bestowed many gifts on him, but still he framed him in such a way that he was able to stand yet able also to fall. To be sure, if he had willed to, God could have created him so complete that he was unable to sin. The condition of the blessed proves this. For in the heavenly land the spirits of the saints, and we ourselves when we will arrive there, will be strengthened so fully that we will be unable to sin any more. Otherwise, that state of blessedness would not be complete; it would be accompanied by a fear of falling. Nevertheless, he did not afford this to Adam.

And since by his foreknowledge he knew that Adam was going to fall, he could have prevented the fall. But he did not will to do this. He willed instead to allow him to fall, and from his eternal decree he had Christ as the remedy for his fall. We cannot explain the others matters concerning that state in specific detail, because we do not have a complete knowledge of it. Let us return to our own condition. As it is before our being made new through Christ, we are unable to will anything good, but of necessity we lie helplessly in sins and cannot raise ourselves up—so far are we from being able to stand in righteousness, as was granted to the first Adam.

But even though, as we have said, God is not properly the cause of sin, still we should not drag him off from his throne as though he does not also rule over sins and heal them. Let us steadfastly affirm this truth within ourselves: that nothing can be done by us or by any creature outside of God's will. And yet let us not excuse our sins on this basis, as though we wished to obey God's will by sinning. We ought to censure ourselves, since we find the beginnings of sin in ourselves. As far as God's will is concerned, we should follow what Scripture teaches and not fall away from his law. And when we sometimes do fall away from it, we should reckon that the motion of turning away from God and turning toward the lusts of the world belongs to our will in its current corrupted state, not as it was created by God. Thus, there are deficient causes of that motion, but we ought not to seek an efficient cause which has God too as a cooperator. Hence we observe that in the book of Genesis darkness is not said to have been made by God. It says, "Darkness was over the face of the abyss" [Gen. 1:2], but God controlled it so that it prevailed at night. It was a privation. In the same way, this motion of turning away from God, since it falls short and deprives men's actions of the appropriate goodness, is indeed a cause, but a deficient one.

[CHAPTER 8: THE DEFORMITY OF SIN INHERES IN THE WILL]

18. Now that these points have been explained, three topics remain to be discussed. The first will concern the guilt of sins, or liability to punishment; the second will concern the subject of deformity or privation, that is, the very act of human will; the third, which is also generally received, is that sin is a punishment of sin, and whether sin can be said to depend on God under these three respects.

As far as the first one is concerned, we should know that a deformed and corrupt act is in some respect the foundation for the punishment that is due. For the apostle says, "The wages of sin is death" [Rom. 6:23], and when we sin, there arises a liability to bear the punishment for the wicked act that has been committed. That guilt is said to arise from divine justice, insofar as God wills to render to each one what is due to him. But no obligation arises unless there is or has been sin. Therefore, we grant that a just occasion for the liability to punishment comes from sinning. Hence, if by sin we mean the guilt and the liability, we do not doubt that this comes from God as an efficient cause. But these things should not properly be called sin, since they pertain to justice. Nevertheless, sometimes they are so called, as when God is said to remit, to blot out, or to absolve sins. For he does not make it so that they do not exist or did not exist, and of course the evil motions remain in us, but the liability to bear the punishment for the wicked act that has been committed is done away with. This liability, as we said, pertains to justice and is a good thing.

19. In the second place we must consider the subject itself in which the deformity of sin inheres. If we are to speak about this as the case actually is, we will not be afraid to say that God is the cause. For the action itself is a species of natural thing, and whatever exists, insofar as it exists, is brought into being not only by creatures but through God, seeing that, as Scripture says, "All things were made through him" [John 1:3]. The universalizing term embraces absolutely all things that exist, in whatever way they exist, insofar as they exist. Augustine says, near the beginning of his book *On the Manichaean Way of Life*, "The Catholic church believes that God is the author of all natures and substances." What he means by *nature* he explained a little before, in these words: "Nature is nothing else than that which something is conceived to be in its own kind."[1] Thus, just as we now call by the new name *essence*—from the fact that it is *to exist* [*esse*]—that which we also very often call *substance*, so the ancients, who did not have these names, used to call it *nature* instead of *essence* and *substance*. Therefore, since the motions of our mind

---

1. Augustine, *De moribus ecclesiae catholicae* 2.2.3, 2.2.2 (*The Catholic and Manichaean Ways of Life*, 66).

are species of things, there is no doubt that in this sense they depend on God.

Indeed God acts as the highest cause, and the creatures cooperate. Hence Anselm wrote in his book *On the Fall of the Devil* that the devil's evil willing itself, insofar as it is a willing, depends on God, and the thing itself is not depraved except insofar as the devil himself wills evilly.[2] But that act is a species of thing, as is clear from the fact that it is in the genus or predicament *action*. Therefore, inasmuch as it is a particular thing, it is from God and is a creature. In fact, Augustine said in *On the Trinity*, book 9, chapter 10, that the accidents of the mind are more excellent than those of bodies, due to the nobility of the subject.[3] Hence form or beauty, as it is in the mind, is nobler than it is as found outwardly in the body. Likewise, the soul itself, being a soul, is still nobler than any body no matter how corrupted it has become. Therefore, the mind's acts, in which privation inheres later on due to our vice, do not come into being without God, insofar as they are things. Anselm said in the passage already cited that God himself is the producer of things, not only of substantial but also of accidental ones, of universal and individual ones, and of motions of the will, even evil ones.[4]

Indeed, God's power is infinite; therefore, nothing of any kind can be produced without being subject to his action. For if anything were to evade his power, then it would not be infinite; it would not fill all things. And our

---

2. Anselm, *De casu diaboli* 20 (*PL* 158:351–52).

3. Augustine, *De trinitate* 9.11.16 (*On the Trinity*, *NPNF* 1/3:132).

4. Anselm, *De casu diaboli* 20 (*PL* 158:352).

will could not[5] break out into act if that highest will were not acting along with it. Augustine in *On True Religion*, chapter 34, writes as follows: "Existence as such, in however small a degree, is a good, since the supreme existence is the supreme good."[6] A little later: "The supreme species is the supreme good; the lowest species is the lowest good, and yet it is a good."[7] Hence, if that action of which are speaking pertains to being in any way, it is something good. Therefore, if sin is under discussion, we need to make a distinction and to note what positive element is there, as they say in the schools,[8] and we must first consider the subject itself; but, on the other hand, we must consider what element of defect and privation inheres in it. But in privation itself, when we see a defect, it is not an efficient cause that we must seek but a deficient cause of it. But the positive element which is found there has need of an efficient cause, and the highest of all efficient causes is God.

20. But a serious misgiving crops up. There are certain sins which are called sins of omission, and in them there does not seem to be an act or work of the will that is a substrate in which defect or privation could inhere. Rather, whatever is in them seems to be privation. A per-

---

5. *Nec* Heidelberg 1603: *Ne* Samuel 1564, London 1576, Zurich 1580.

6. Augustine, *De vera religione* 18.35 (*Of True Religion*, 242).

7. Augustine, *De vera religione* 18.35 (*Of True Religion*, 242).

8. The reference is to the scholastic distinction between the "positive" and "privative" elements in sin; see Aquinas, *Summa Theologiae* I q. 86 a. 1 arg. 3 and ad 3; a. 2 ad 1.

son is said to omit his duty because he does not do what he ought. For example, if someone does not love his neighbor, or if someone does not come to the sacred assembly to hear the word of God and partake of the sacraments, there seems to be only privation in this sin, without any definable act that could be its underlying subject. Some people reply that even in that instance we should seek for a nature or an action, a work or thing, to be the subject underlying the privation, and they say that will is what is lacking. For inasmuch as will itself is nature, a will that sins is preserved in the order it has from God—but not insofar as it sins.

This solution can be tolerated,[9] but when I examine the issue more attentively something else seems to be the case. I see an act in those sins of omission. For sometimes that omission of one's duty occurs upon consideration. Then that corrupt man wills not to love his neighbor or wills not to go to the sacred assembly. So we see here an act of the will. And insofar as[10] that action of will is an action of nature, it depends on God, but deformity and privation do not have this dependence. But sometimes the actions are omitted because someone is not thinking about those things, not out of contempt. Here I say that even if in such cases there is no action of this kind, still there is another action that is inconsistent with right reason. He is not thinking about the sacred assembly because he wishes to go on a walk or to play, and those actions are inconsistent with right activity. Or if there is no such action at that

---

9. *Ferri* Samuel 1564, London 1576, Zurich 1580: *Fieri* Heidelberg 1603.

10. *qua* Samuel 1564, London 1576, Zurich 1580: *quae* Heidelberg 1603.

time, there was one a little earlier. For instance, at night he wished to immerse himself in pleasure; later he was not able to rise early in the morning to be at the sacred assembly. Thus, we will find an action in sins of omission: either an action that is proper to that type, or another action that is inconsistent with a good motion of the will—whether it is maintained at that time or whether it took place before.

21. Therefore, God is the cause of all things; but lower things receive the motion of the first cause in keeping with their nature. So if a fault is incurred, it is incurred by the nature of the second causes. I will illustrate this fact with a simile. In living things we find a power which is called the power of locomotion, and it moves animals either to walking or to running. But they move inasmuch as they receive the motion from the locomotive power. However, if a leg is injured, put out of joint, or crooked, that motion is accompanied by a limping of movement. But that limping, inasmuch as it is a motion, is from the motive faculty of the mind; inasmuch as it is faulty and lame, it depends on the fault in the leg that has been broken. So it is with that constant motion of God by which he moves his creatures to action. There is indeed a common influence, and it is received in things according to their quality. In this way the subject of deformity or privation is from God, and the motion of God sometimes passes through a depraved mind. Hence the fault in the action is not incurred from God but from the nearest cause. But what God does in that case, and how he directs that deformity, has been explained above; at present we are discussing the act that issues forth from our will.

So it is rightly said that privation of rightness does not follow the work and motion of our will insofar as it is in the genus of nature but inasmuch as it is in the genus of motion. Augustine in *On the City of God*, book 7, chapter 30, says that God manages creatures in such a way that he allows them to exercise their own movements as co-agents.[11] For God does not act alone, but, as I said above, wicked men and the devil bring their own wickedness to bear in the acting. But when we say that the very action which afterward is evil due to our vice is brought about by the supreme cause, that is, God, and by us, that is, by our will, how shall we understand this? Is it that God does the whole thing and we do the whole thing? Or that he does part and we do part? And here we confine the production to that very act of our will. Our response is this: We must speak in one way if the explanation for the whole[12] be referred to the cause, in a different way if it be referred to the effect. If the whole be referred to the cause, such that we understand our will to be the whole cause of the action, so that it can produce through itself apart from God, it is not true, because it could not produce the action if God did not give his assent. And so, even though God by his absolute power could accomplish the work through his own self, yet in the actual course of things he does not will to act alone; instead he wills to have a creature as co-agent. In this way, neither the will nor God is said to be the whole cause. But if the explanation be referred to the effect itself, God and the will are the complete cause, for God and the will produce the whole effect, even though they are

---

11. Augustine, *De civitate dei* 7.30 (*City of God*, NPNF 1/2:140).

12. *toti* Samuel 1564, London 1576, Zurich 1580: *totius* Heidelberg 1603.

conjoined in the action. I will explain this fact by an example. We have the will and the intelligence to produce an action, and the will brings about the whole effect and the intelligence is the cause of the whole effect. But the one cause is close, the other more remote. So it is with the will and God. The will itself brings about the whole and God brings about the whole, but the one cause is primary, the other secondary.

[CHAPTER 9: SINS CAN BE PUNISHMENTS FOR OTHER SINS]

22. As far as the third point is concerned, a later sin is sometimes said to be the punishment for an earlier sin, and so God is said to punish sins by means of sins. If then the later sins are thought of as punishments, they are ascribed to God in some sense—not because he instills a new wickedness, or directly impels people to commit sin, but because once he has withdrawn his gifts, sin then follows and ravages the mind. And those ravagings and woundings of our minds happen to us justly inasmuch as they are punishments. On this subject, it is written in the letter to the Romans, first chapter [v. 28], that God[1] handed them over to a reprobate mind, in the way we already explained earlier. Now it is clear that sin has the character of punishment, because it corrupts nature. Augustine says, and it is an oft-repeated saying, "You have ordained, Lord, and so it truly is the case, that every sin is a punishment of the

---

1. *Deus* Samuel 1564, London 1576, Zurich 1580: *Deum* Heidelberg 1603.

sinner."[2] Even the pagans recognize this. Horace says, "The Sicilian tyrants invented no greater torment than envy."[3] Those depraved affections dry up the marrow, sap people's strength, and impair their minds. But this happens justly. For God is just and right in all his ways. But if we are deprived of grace, we have deserved this.

23. So we bring this inquiry of ours to a close and we say that, properly and unqualifiedly speaking, God is not the cause of sin, nor does he will sin. Yet God is not said to be more imperfect or weaker due to his inability to bring about sin, for this is not imperfection and powerlessness but perfection. God is incapable of these things because he is the highest good and highest perfection. And in fact he lays down laws against sins; he cries out against them and punishes them. Nor should you be surprised when I said that God cannot properly will sin, because then he would be able to turn men away from himself, and in that case he would deny himself to be God. In the letter to Timothy it is said, "God cannot deny himself" [2 Tim. 2:13].

This is the reason that in his booklet *On Precept and Dispensation* Bernard was moved to say that God can loosen something from the precepts of the second table but not of the first.[4] He loosened something from the second table, for instance, when he wills for Abraham to slay his own son; so too when he orders the Israelites to carry off other people's goods. But the precepts that belong to the

---

2. Augustine, *Confessiones* 1.12.19 (*Confessions*, NPNF 1/1:51).

3. Horace, *Epistles* 1.2.58–59.

4. Bernard of Clairvaux, *De praecepto et dispensatione* 3.6 (*On Precept and Dispensation*, 109).

first table cannot be relaxed, for then God would be denying himself, if he did not will to be worshipped and loved. If he is the highest good, is it not our duty to love and worship him?

Some bring forward the argument that those goods which pertain to one's neighbor are particular, and God can take away some private good in order to replace it with a greater one. By contrast, the things that pertain to his worship have the principle of a universal good, and therefore they cannot be done away with. Augustine says, in the book which is entitled *Catholic Refutation of Certain Opinions Falsely Attributed to Him*, chapter 3, "Anything that is condemned in anyone is repugnant to the author of nature."[5] Likewise: "It is a damnable opinion which holds that God is the author of any evil action or evil will."[6]

---

5. The work from which this quotation and the following one come is actually Prosper of Aquitaine, *Pro Augustino responsiones ad capitula obiectionum Vincentianarum* 3.resp. (*PL* 51:179). Prosper (c.390–c.455 AD) was a correspondent and student of Augustine and a vigorous champion of Augustine's doctrines of grace and free will against Pelagianism in Gaul.

6. Prosper of Aquitaine, *Pro Augustino responsiones ad capitula obiectionum Vincentianarum* 10.resp. (*PL* 51:182).

[CHAPTER 10: THE CAUSES OF SIN SUMMARIZED]

24. The proper causes of sin have now been shown in general terms. But if we must treat them one by one, we posit that the cause of sin is human will, intellect, depraved affections, the sensitive appetite, the apparent good which presents itself (for we desire something only under the guise of a good). To this is added the tinder of original sin, from which depraved affections continuously waft forth like the noxious exhalations from a poisonous swamp. Then again, the cause is weakness, ignorance, the suggestion of the devil, the suggestion of evil men; but these can achieve nothing more than God allows. There are bad examples; sin itself is a cause of sin, for a spendthrift steals to satisfy his own appetite. So then, because there are so many genuine causes of sins, it is not right to make God the author of sin in order to excuse ourselves. It can now be apparent that we must condemn the depraved opinion of the Libertines who excuse all sins. As for those who make God the cause of evil but not with the intent that we excuse ourselves, it seems they do not explain this issue

well; the same is true of those who make bare permission the cause.

First, then, to sum up everything in a few words, we have said that God is properly not the author of sin; second, that God, when he wills, justly removes his grace, which was preventing sin. In addition to this, we posited that God guides sins by his own providence in such a way that they proceed no farther than he himself allows, nor in any other way than is expedient for his providence. We have shown that God sometimes suggests, inwardly and outwardly, things that are good of their own nature but that, if they meet with corrupt men, become occasions of sins that are taken, not given. Again: that God does not hinder but permits sins; nevertheless, such permission is not at all independent of God's will. And that, since sin is a defect and privation, it does not need an efficient cause but a deficient one. Again, that the motion of moving away from God is proper to the will insofar as[1] it has been corrupted but not inasmuch as it was created by God. We have said also that guilt depends on God, and also that the action which is the subject of deformity comes both from God and from us in its own genus of cause. Likewise, that sins are punished by other sins. And lastly we enumerated the genuine causes of sins.

---

1. *qua* Samuel 1564, London 1576, Zurich 1580: *quae* Heidelberg 1603.

[CHAPTER 11: ARGUMENTS THAT GOD IS NOT THE CAUSE OF SIN ARE ANSWERED]

25. But now we will scrutinize the arguments already presented above. Those who denied that God is the cause of sin, as we also assert, made use of these arguments. The first is: Augustine said in his *Book of Eighty-Three Questions*, question 3, "A wise man is not the author of anything that causes a person to become worse; therefore, neither is God."[1] We grant this, for it is not by virtue of God's having given the law that a person becomes worse, seeing that he does not command evil things in his own law. Nor does a person become worse in view of a natural act which God brings about. Rather, he becomes worse due to a defect, the deficient causes of which we possess in our own selves. And thus the devil, wicked men, our own lust, and above all our corrupted will make us worse. Therefore, we grant that we are not at all made worse by God or by man.

---

1. Augustine, *De diversis quaestionibus octoginta tribus* 3 (*Eighty-Three Different Questions*, 37–38); Vermigli compresses Augustine's syllogism here.

The second argument is: Fulgentius says, "God is not an avenger of things of which he is the author."[2] We grant the argument: God does not avenge that act inasmuch as it is a natural thing, inasmuch as it depends on himself; and he does not avenge his own governance which he brings to bear, but rather the depravity which depends on us and comes from us.

The third is: God does not hate the things he makes, but he does hate sin. The argument is solid, but a question remains: If he truly hates sin, why does he not prevent it when he could do so? Human reason can scarcely discern God's perfect hatred against sin, because he does not do away with sin itself. It is indeed a difficulty. But it often happens that, instead of doing away with something that displeases him, one turns it to some good end. In human affairs, examples are not lacking. Someone is in an ill condition with his body; secretions break out so that an ulcer is formed on one of his limbs, which is very displeasing. Yet because he realizes that it will be beneficial for him, he puts up with the annoyance and does not block the ulcer. Similarly, chaff grows up along with the wheat; it is displeasing, but it is not gotten rid of, because people are worried that the wheat may get uprooted. We could say the same of God. He has his own ends, namely that not only his goodness but also his justice may be manifested. For this reason he hates sins, yet not in such

---

2. Fulgentius, *Ad Monimum* 1.19 (*PL* 65:167). Fulgentius's text, however, says something else: "God is an avenger of that thing of which he is not the author." Aquinas quotes the Fulgentius passage to the same effect as Augustine in his *Commentary on the Sentences*, 2.32.2.2.arg.5, and *Quaestiones disputatae de potentia dei*, 3.6.arg.23.

a way that he does not will through them to obtain his foreordained end.

Other arguments: If he were making sin he would be a sinner, and if he induced us to sin he would be acting contrary to his own nature. After all, natural things in their activity strive to make the thing they do similar to themselves, etc. These arguments are firm; God's action and the cooperation of the creature—that is, of human will—should not be framed in such a way that we ourselves do not bring our own wickedness to bear.

God would seem to be acting hypocritically if he commanded good things on the one hand but willed sin on the other. I reply that this argument would be sound if God were said to impart new wickedness; but the fact that he governs sin does not imply his doing anything contrary to his own law. Moreover, we must make a distinction about the will of God as it relates to commands and to men. We call written commands the will of God because they express his nature and mind. But if we were to observe how God's will relates to men, and to say that God equally wills to propel all men to observe his commands and gives grace to them all equally, this should not be granted. For God has his own elect, as well as others whom he passes over in his just judgment and abandons to sin and destruction. The Lord says, "I will have compassion on whom I will have compassion" [Rom. 9:15], that is, on whomever I will be pleased to have compassion.

But they say that men have free choice, so that they can observe God's law if they wish, and no distinction should be posited within God's help and grace, which is not granted to all in the same way. But I posit[3] free choice in God: he is free in his election and in distributing graces, but his freedom does not depend on us, who will be truly free if the Son will set us free [John 8:36]. Therefore, in the law, or commands, God shows what his mind is and what things he judges to be right. But as for the favor with which he attends individual men so that they observe these things, that is a different question.

It was said in 2 Chronicles [36:15; cf. Jer. 7:25] that God rose at early morning and sent his prophets; therefore, he is not the cause of sin. It is absolutely true that God did this. But the suggestions that were good by their own nature were meeting with men who were evil by nature, and because of their own vice they were being made worse by those admonitions, for they were incited by their own guilt to commit sin. God was giving such warnings for the purpose of sparing his own people, and the warnings were such that once accepted they would bring forgiveness with them. But we ought not to say that God's decree at that time was to save them absolutely. For he had justly withdrawn his grace from them, but they were neither able nor willing through themselves to comply with the prophets' warnings.

The Son of God wept over the destruction of Jerusalem [Matt. 23:37], and this event took place because of their sins; therefore, God does not will sins. I grant that sins are not done by the will of God, properly speaking.

---

3. *pono* Samuel 1564, London 1576, Zurich 1580: *non pono* Heidelberg 1603.

What then was he weeping over?[4] He was now our neighbor; he could not help being grieved by the evils of his neighbors. Likewise, he realized that sin was contrary to God's will, even though he was aware that sin could not happen outside of God's will.

26. It is written in the prophet Hosea, "Your destruction is from yourself, Israel, but your salvation is from me" [13:9]. This is a perfectly true statement, for since sins are from us as their proper causes, destruction is from us. Guilt, or the liability to bear punishment, can be said to be from God. But this, as we showed above, is not properly called sin. Rather, it pertains to justice.

John 8 [v. 44]: "When the devil speaks falsehood, he speaks from his own." It is perfectly true: God does not instill wickedness in the devil. Yet he is accustomed to make use of the devil's lies, as he does with other things.

In Jeremiah we read, "They were running and I was not sending them" [23:21]. In that passage he is not discussing the providence of God, but the wickedness of the false prophets, who were pretending that they had received a word from God but were fully aware in themselves that God had not spoken. They were saying they had dreamed a dream and were babbling that they had received some revelation from God, but they were lying and knew that they were lying. And so no reproaches should be leveled against God on this account, as if he were not allowed to use their lies according to his providence.

"This is their condemnation: that the light came into the world, but men loved the darkness more than the

---

4. *flebat* Samuel 1564, London 1576, Zurich 1580: *fiebat* Heidelberg 1603.

light" [John 3:19]. Therefore, the cause is not God, but the very men who loved the darkness. We grant the argument: man's will, due to his own wickedness, has a motion of turning away from the light and toward the darkness.

It was said that God tempts no one [James 1:13] and that if he were the cause of sin he would tempt people. Here is my verdict on this passage. He is not there discussing just any kind of temptation, for then the statement would not be true. For sometimes God does test his own people[5]—not so that his knowledge may increase, but so that people may come to know him, and others too may recognize how much God has accomplished in them, and may see the grace that has been bestowed on them. Again, there is a certain kind of temptation which we ought to seek after. That is why David says in the Psalm, "Try me; burn my kidneys and my heart" [26:2]. And we must not forget what we established earlier: God sometimes suggests, inwardly and outwardly, things that are good by nature but that are received in keeping with people's character, and those types of temptations ought not to be removed from God. James also speaks of the inward lust which is properly the means of suggesting evil things and which incites us to act against God's law [James 4:1–3]. Such lust does not depend on God, except insofar as he does not stand in its way, just as he does not always block the devil.

It was added that God could seem to be acting tyrannically. My response to this is that he does not properly

---

5. The Latin verb used here and in the Psalm passage below, *tento/tempto*, can mean *try* or *test* as well as *tempt*. Similarly, the noun translated *temptation* below can also mean *testing*.

incite people to commit sin, yet he uses the sins of evil men and also governs them so that they do not progress beyond bounds.

It was added: "How could he judge the world? For if he were the author of sin, he would be judging himself." We affirm that God will judge the world justly. For the sin that people commit against God's law is done willingly and voluntarily, not under compulsion, and the Spirit of God will convict the world about judgment, about sin, etc. [John 16:8].

It was also inferred that the logical conclusion would be that in God there are two wills that are at odds with each other. We reply that, as far as God's nature is concerned, the will in God, which is his essence and nature, is simple and unified. However, if we then consider its various objects, it can be said to be manifold. As far as his commands are concerned, his will is just, good, and unified; but insofar as it relates to men, his will propels some while justly depriving others of his favor. And they are not at odds, because they do not deal with the same thing, whereas things that are at odds must involve the same subject. A father has two sons; he wants one of them to study letters, the other not. Are there two wills in the father? No. There is one will, and he is acting rightly, provided that he is doing it for a good reason. Moreover, James says in chapter 4 [vv. 13–15], "You say, 'We will go into this city': you ought to say, 'If the Lord wills.'" Therefore, God's will has to do not only with law and commands but also with those things that people do every day. And this will is not a will of commands, for such everyday things are not contained in the Decalogue and are, in a certain sense, indifferents. Augustine wrote very beautifully in his *Manual for*

Laurentius, chapter 102, "The omnipotent God, whether through compassion he takes pity on whom he willed or though judgment has judged whomever he willed, does nothing unjustly, and he only ever acts willingly."[6]

Next it was said: If he were the cause of sin, what would be the point of the great number of admonitions and entreaties that he gives through the Son of God, the prophets, and the apostles? We say that these are not applied in vain, but usefully. First, those who admonish, reprove, and exhort are obeying the commands of God who wills for this to be done. You will say, "But I will not progress." The outcome must be entrusted to God. Moreover, these things are profitable for the saints, the predestined. Even if it may not appear right away, still they have their own fruit at some point; indeed, they render the wicked less excusable. On this topic, read Augustine's book *On Rebuke and Grace*, for these objections were levelled against him as well.

27. It was concluded that if matters stood thus, every distinction between good and evil would be abolished; all things would be works of God unqualifiedly, as the Libertines claim. We admit that if God were truly the cause of sins, the Libertines would speak rightly; but their opinion is detestable.

The judgment of consciences would be done away with, and so would internal accusations and repentance. A window would be opened for evil deeds; thanksgiving would be destroyed, for we would rejoice in sin; and God's reputation would be greatly impaired. All these assertions

---

6. Augustine, *Enchiridion* 102 (*Enchiridion*, *NPNF* 1/3:270).

are perfectly true, but they do not pose any hindrance to us, for we do not make God to be truly the cause of sin.

In the last place, it was alleged that God wills all people to be saved. If he wills this, he uses good means, not evil ones. Therefore, he is not the cause of sin. We admit most openly that God is not properly the cause of sin. But as far as this passage is concerned, I affirm with Augustine in his *Manual*, chapter 103, that the sentence should not be taken unqualifiedly, as if there is no one whom God does not will to be saved.[7] This sentence, he says, is interpreted in the following way: God has his own elect from every quality and condition of mankind, so that in this connection he does not have respect to persons; he calls kings and private individuals, free people and slaves, males and females. This interpretation squares very nicely with that passage of Paul. He had ordered them to pray for rulers [1 Tim. 2:1–2]; but someone could have supposed that the condition of rulers is such that salvation is incompatible with it. Not at all, he says: God has his own from every class of men. There he brings forward a similar statement from Matthew chapter 13 [23:23; cf. Luke 11:42]: "You tithe mint,[8] rue, and every herb," meaning, all the sorts of herbs that there are among you, not those that there are in India or Europe; for how could they have tithed the herbs of the whole world?

The author of the book *On the Calling of the Gentiles*, which people attribute to Ambrose, did not disagree with

---

7. Augustine, *Enchiridion* 103 (*Enchiridion*, NPNF 1/3:270).

8. *mentam* Zurich 1580, Heidelberg 1603: *mentem* Samuel 1564: *metam* London 1576.

this sentiment, for he says that God has his own totality.[9] And so he judges that this universal proposition must be restricted, so that God is said to will the salvation of those who come within the scope of his own company and number—just as when[10] it is said, "They will all be taught of God [θεοδιδακτούς]" [Isa. 54:13]; and, "All flesh will see the salvation of God" [Luke 3:6]. Another way in which Augustine explains this verse can be found in the same passage. He says, "We understand that no one will be saved whom God does not will to save."[11] It is as if you were to say, "There is a grammarian at Tigurum[12] who teaches everyone grammar." He does not teach all the citizens, but there is no one who is taught grammar who is not taught by him. And this is how he understands the statement, "He enlightens everyone coming into this world" [John 1:9]: that is, all who are enlightened are enlightened by this Word.

But, he says, it is not true that God wills all people to be saved unqualifiedly. For in Matthew 11 [v. 21] it is written, "Woe to you, Chorazin; woe to you, Bethsaida. For if the mighty deeds that were done among you had been done in the city of Tyre or Sidon, they would long

---

9. In Latin, *universitas*. The reference is to Prosper of Aquitaine, *De vocatione omnium gentium* 1.9 (*The Call of All Nations*, 46), a work against the Semi-Pelagians. Its authorship was long disputed, and some fifteenth- and sixteenth-century editors anachronistically attributed it to Ambrose.

10. *cum* Samuel 1564, London 1576: *om.* Zurich 1580, Heidelberg 1603.

11. Augustine, *Enchiridion* 103 (*Enchiridion*, NPNF 1/3:270).

12. That is, Zurich.

ago have repented of their wicked deeds in sackcloth and ashes." Christ was unwilling to perform mighty deeds of miracles among them, who, he said, would have repented if they had been performed. And he adds, "Let it be explained in whatever way, provided we are not forced to believe that the omnipotent God willed for something to happen and it did not happen, since the Truth sings, 'He has done all things whatever he has willed in the heavens and on earth' [Psalm 115:3]; and obviously he did not do what he did not will."[13] Let this suffice concerning the arguments made to the first part.

---

13. Augustine, *Enchiridion* 103 (*Enchiridion*, *NPNF* 1/3:271).

[CHAPTER 12: ARGUMENTS THAT GOD IS THE CAUSE OF SIN ARE ANSWERED]

28. Now let us take up the arguments of those who say that God is the cause of evil. In the letter to the Romans 1 [v. 28], it is said that God handed them over to a reprobate mind. The interpretation is easy: he handed them over to the desires of their own heart, as he himself explains later. Thus, those desires were already evil. What did God do? He allowed them to follow the promptings of the evil desires. He did not do evil things; but when he deprived them of his grace, the desires which were evil prevailed in them (privation follows of itself). Nevertheless, God used their corrupted desires in order to bring his justice to pass, namely by punishing them. As for the hardening of Pharaoh, it was sufficiently explained above.

Isaiah 6 [vv. 9–10], when God says through the prophet, "Blind their heart so that hearing they may not hear and seeing they may not understand," etc. There are two ways of explaining this. Jerome, to interpret these words,[1] draws on the passage from chapter 11 of the let-

---

1. Jerome, *Commentarii in Isaiam prophetam* 3.6.9–10 (*PL* 24:101).

ter to the Romans [vv. 30–31] where it is said concerning the Gentile nations and the Hebrews, "At one time the Gentiles were unbelieving while you believed, but now they have obtained mercy as a result of your unbelief." While the Gentiles were not believing, the Jews seemed to have the true worship. On the other hand, later on when preaching was tendered to them, they did not believe. The apostles left them behind and turned to the Gentiles. Thus, they were destined to be unbelieving in order that the Gentiles might be admitted into grace. So God was using that unbelief of the Jews; and that is why he adds, "God has shut up all under unbelief in order that he may have mercy on all" [Rom. 11:32]. Therefore, that blinding of the unbelieving was destined to serve the purpose of divine providence, as the prophet predicts.

There can be another interpretation, which is more fitting. God willed to commission Isaiah to preach, but lest he should later become terrified when he saw that they were stubborn and received the word as a stumbling block, God informs him in advance that this is going to happen. The word of God does not have this effect of itself, but he justly withdrew his Spirit and grace from them. "This word of yours," he says, "will be an occasion taken, so that they become more blind and are estranged from me." We should understand this as applying to the majority, for there were some good individuals among them. And it is declared that this will happen for the following end: that in their perishing they may manifest the justice of God, who willed to use this blindness of theirs by his own just judgment. But as for the blindness being from God, we should understand this to be true only in regard to outward things, for he was supplying his word to them through Isaiah.

29. Another passage: "Do not lead us into temptation" [Matt. 6:13]. It is worded as if God does lead some people into temptation and thus is the cause of sin. Augustine interprets this saying of the Lord in his booklet *On Nature and Grace*, chapter 58: "We pray that we may resist the devil in order that the devil may flee when we say, 'Do not bring us into temptation.' Thus we are also admonished, as if we were soldiers addressed by a general exhorting and saying, 'Be on your guard and pray, that you may not enter into temptation' [Matt. 26:41]."[2] Thus Augustine there attributes these things to the temptation of the devil, who can accomplish nothing except insofar as God has permitted. And in chapter 67 of the same book he adds, "We can guard against bodily diseases in two ways: either to keep them from occurring, or to be quickly freed from them if they do occur."[3] Therefore, when we say "Do not bring us into temptation," we will for God to avert sin so that it does not happen. But if we have slipped up and committed sin, then we ask him to remit and forgive it.

The same author, in *Against Two Letters of Pelagius*, book 4, chapter 9, writes, quoting the testimony of Cyprian, "When it is said, 'Do not bring us into temptation,' we are apprised of our weakness and infirmity. For the Lord says, 'Be on your guard and pray, that you may not enter into temptation.' The explanation is added—'The spirit is

---

2. Augustine, *De natura et gratia* 58.68 (*On Nature and Grace*, NPNF 1/5:145).

3. Augustine, *De natura et gratia* 67.80 (*On Nature and Grace*, NPNF 1/5:149).

willing, but the flesh is weak' [Matt. 26:41]—so that we may not arrogantly puff ourselves up."[4] Here temptation is ascribed to fleshly weakness, in such a way that God is excluded from being the author. In his book *On the Good of Perseverance*, chapter 6, he says that Cyprian inserts that word into the quotation, "Do not *allow* us to be led into temptation," because he sees that the devil is capable of no more than God has permitted to him.[5] But as far as his own are concerned, God ensures that the devil does not get the upper hand. In the case of the wicked, on the contrary, if he gets the upper hand, God cannot be blamed—unless we should say that he is to be blamed for having not hindered evils and for directing them and using them in the service of his providence.

At this point we were raising the objection that it is hardly possible for punishment and fault to be the same thing. After all, sin is so called in respect of its being voluntary, whereas punishment is always inflicted on the unwilling; and how can it make sense for the same thing to be voluntary and involuntary? We reply that we can consider our will in two ways, as far as sin is concerned. In one way, as that from which sin proceeds and by which it is brought about, and in this sense it is called a voluntary thing. In another way, sin is considered as being in the mind or will and deforming it, and in this sense it cannot be voluntary. For no depraved persons would will for their own mind to

---

4. Augustine, *Contra duas epistulas Pelagianorum* 4.9.25 (*Against Two Letters of the Pelagians*, NPNF 1/5:428), citing Cyprian's *De oratione dominica* 14 (*On the Lord's Prayer*, ANF 5:454).

5. Augustine, *De dono perseverantiae* 6.12 (*On the Gift of Perseverance*, NPNF 1/5:530).

be corrupted, wounded, or destroyed. Therefore, insofar as sin is produced by the will as an effective cause, it is voluntary, but insofar as it imports a stain, it happens contrary to the will; for all of us would will to be whole.

It was added that God is the cause of the cause of sin; therefore, he is also the cause of sin. What are the things by which we sin? The will and the affections, which God has brought into being. Therefore, he is also the cause of the last effect. We reply that sin does not depend on the will and affections insofar as these were created by God, but as they are in their current vitiated state. We brought forward an analogy above involving lameness.

30. In addition to this, we were saying that God removes his grace and Spirit which prevent sin; therefore, etc. We admit this; but we add that he removes his Spirit justly. He is indeed *a cause that removes the obstacle*, but that is not the proper cause, seeing that there are also inward causes of evils in us. He gives occasions, it is true; he makes suggestions inwardly and outwardly; but he suggests good things, which people make an evil use of because of their own vice.

But he does not merely give occasions—he also uttered commands. He said to the devil, "Go out; do it." I will make just a few observations on this point. Through the figure of prosopopoeia,[6] the prophet introduces God as sitting on a throne like a judge. He wills for Ahab to be killed; he seeks for someone to deceive him. What is the meaning of that search? He implies that this is being sought from another source, because it is not in the divine

---

6. *Prosopopoeia* is a figure of speech in which an absent figure is introduced as speaking.

nature to deceive. There the end is set out by his justice: he wills for Ahab to now be killed. Different methods are proposed. This spirit was saying this thing, another spirit another, to the end that we might understand that God's providence has countless ways in which it can punish people. These ways are proposed there, but they are not described, because providence did not will to use them. A spirit came forward and said, "I will deceive him" [1 Kings 22:19–22]. We gather that the devils are readily inclined to deceive, and when they deceive they act from their own resources. Meanwhile, we are taught that those spirits cannot act except inasmuch as God has permitted and insofar as he wills to make use of them: they are God's executors. It is for this reason that God says "Go out": this is the imperative mood, if we refer it to the end, namely that Ahab be killed and punished. But insofar as the devil had to exercise an evil will and deceive, this was a concession, and God was making use of the devil's sin and willing to not block his action and to not prevent Ahab from believing the false prophets. Augustine in his *Book of Eighty-Three Questions*, question 53, made three observations.[7] First, what God did against Ahab he did by way of judgment. Secondly, he did it through an angel, not through himself. Thirdly, Augustine says, not through just any angel but through an evil angel, one prepared by his own nature to deceive.

It was asserted that sin is a motion and a kind of action, and that God is the first mover. No conclusion follows from this except that the subject of sin, that is, the

---

7. Augustine, *De diversis quaestionibus octoginta tribus* 53.2 (*Eighty-Three Different Questions*, 92).

act itself, has the will as its proximate cause, and also God, insofar as it is a natural thing. Augustine's opinion, in *On Grace and Free Choice*, chapter 21, has been explained concerning [the will's] being inclined to good through itself but to evil indirectly.[8]

Also the action of Rehoboam, and the stirring up of the Philistines, and Amaziah's unwillingness to obey the admonitions of the prophet of the king of Israel, come within the scope of God's justice: God willed to punish them. As for the word of Ahijah the Shilonite, "that it might be fulfilled," etc. [1 Kings 12:15], these things were not done because they had been foretold, but they were foretold because God foresaw that they would happen. And in order that they might happen thus, he had appointed them for the punishment of evil men, and he knew how he willed to make use of them, and God had his own fixed reasons.

Ezekiel 14 [v. 9]: "If a prophet had been enticed," etc. Here we learn nothing except that the sin of the false prophets can be considered in two ways. Insofar as it proceeds from the will of an evil prophet, it displeases God, and for this reason he said that he would punish that prophet. But if afterward one considers the use, namely that God willed to inflict retribution on the people by this enticement, he was justly withdrawing his grace from that prophet; then also he was using this enticement, which cannot be ascribed to God through itself and properly.

31. The passage from Proverbs 21 [v. 1] was brought forward, where it was said that the king's heart is in the

---

8. Augustine, *De gratia et libero arbitrio* 21.42–43 (*On Grace and Free Choice*, 178–80).

hand of God and that he inclines it wherever he has willed. It is a universal proposition: he inclines it wherever he has willed; there is no exception. Therefore, he inclines it equally to good things and to evil ones. In Job chapter 12 [vv. 24–25] we are told that God takes away the heart from those who hold sway over the earth and makes them stagger like drunken men. I have explained how these things ought to be understood of inclination. And so I understand that statement of Solomon no differently than those words of Augustine in *On Grace and Free Choice*: that he inclines our wills to good or to evil in keeping with his own good pleasure.[9]

Another argument was from Psalm 104 where it is said, "God turned their heart so that they hated them" [Psalm 105:25]. In that passage, Augustine clearly teaches what is that turning which he brought about in their heart.[10] It was not a good heart which God made evil; rather, the goodness of God is such that he makes use of angels and men, and when they are evil, he extracts good things from them. He enriched the Israelites with children and wealth; those were good things. Thus, by doing good to the Hebrews, God turned their heart to envy, for envy has the prosperity of others as its object. Therefore, God turned their heart, which was evil of its own accord,[11] to hatred of the Hebrews—not by making their heart evil.

---

9. Augustine, *De gratia et libero arbitrio* 21.43 (*On Grace and Free Choice*, 180–81).

10. Augustine, *De gratia et libero arbitrio* 21.42 (*On Grace and Free Choice*, 180).

11. *sponte malum* Samuel 1564, London 1576: *malum sponte* Zurich 1580, Heidelberg 1603.

Arguments that God Is the Cause of Sin Are Answered

So you see that I was not fabricating when I said that God suggests things that are good by their own nature, either inwardly or outwardly, but that because of our vice become occasions of sinning—but occasions taken, not given. And the occasions that are suggested are not extremely remote causes, like a fir tree felled on Mount Pelion, but they are immediate occasions which rouse our lusts, just as the prosperity of the Hebrews was an immediate occasion for the envy of the Egyptians.

Isaiah 63 [v. 17]: "Why have you led us astray, Lord?" Jerome interprets this of God's indulgence.[12] For God was not punishing sins immediately, and consequently they began to despise God's judgments. God was offering them this mercy of his, which was good; but because of their vice it was swept along to contempt. They could also be the words of wicked men, who transfer the cause of their own sins to God. Or upright men, who reflect that they have been forsaken of grace by God in his just judgment and who afterward recognize their own sins and speak these words—not by way of rebuking God, to be sure, but in admiration of his judgments. But however you understand it, God is exempted from blame.

Jeremiah 4 [v. 10]: "Alas, you have led your people astray." Jerome replies: The things that were now being spoken seemed to the prophet to be inconsistent with what had been said in the third chapter, where God had revealed to the prophet that Jerusalem would be called God's throne and that all nations would flow to it. But now God was saying that the king and the rulers would

---

12. Jerome, *Commentarii in Isaiam prophetam* 17.63.18–19 (*PL* 24:643).

lose heart, that the priests and people would be stunned. For this reason the prophet cries out, "You said there would be peace, but behold, a sword." But Jerome says that we must make a distinction regarding the times. For the words that were spoken earlier were to be fulfilled after the Babylonian captivity, whereas the tribulation which was announced later was at the doors.[13]

32. Joshua says that God hardened the hearts of those Canaanite nations so that they did not make peace with the Israelites, because God was willing to destroy them [Josh. 11:19–20]; therefore, he himself seems to be the cause of sin. We reply with Augustine, from chapter 8 of *On Grace and Predestination*, which is also titled *A Book on the Will of God*: "What is it to harden? To will not to soften. What is it to blind? To will not to illuminate. What is it to compel or reject? To will not to call."[14] He says this not about general calling but about efficacious calling. God does not instill a new hardness that is not present in the heart. Therefore, it will be said that God hardened those nations because he was willing not to soften them so they would make peace with the Hebrews; however, they were already going to be destroyed on account of their own sins.

But the objection is raised: No creature was destined for this end, to wind up in destruction. God did not create man in order to cast him away. And Jerome is quoted as saying, in *On the Prophet Habakkuk*, chapter 2, "Even if

---

13. Jerome, *Commentarii in Ieremiam prophetam* 1.4.10 (*PL* 24:735).

14. The quote actually comes from Pseudo-Fulgentius, *Liber de praedestinatione et gratia* 4 (*PL* 65:845).

through its own vice the soul becomes a lodging-place of the Chaldeans, still by its own nature it is a tabernacle of God, and no rational creature was made for this end, to be a habitation for demons."[15] I reply: He does say this, but if you take it without qualification, it would conflict with Scripture, which speaks otherwise. It says that the potter has power to make out of the same lump a vessel of glory and a vessel of disgrace. And it is said of Pharaoh, "I raised you up for this purpose: that I might manifest my own power." God endures vessels fitted for destruction in order to manifest his own power [Rom. 9:17, 21–23]. It is also said through Solomon in Proverbs 16 [v. 4] that the wicked man has been made for the evil day. In the letter of Jude [v. 4] mention is made of certain men who had long been marked out for this judgment or for this condemnation. It is indeed true that this decree of God, before it finds execution, has just grounds for condemning any person. For sins happen in the meantime which justify the condemnation of the damned. However, it is the decree of God that he does not call them efficaciously, and that decree is undoubtedly just. But as far as Jerome himself is concerned, I reply that the rational creature was not made for the purpose of being compelled; he sins by his own vice; nevertheless, it is in the decree of God not to prevent that vice of the creature.

I further reply, like Zwingli in his booklet *On the Providence of God*, chapter 6: It would follow that God procures thefts and other such things. "Go even further," he says, "and you would assert that this happens in order

---

15. Jerome, *Commentarii in Abacuc prophetam* 1.1.6–11 (*PL* 25:1280).

to manifest his justice."[16] Then we see for what purpose the rational creature was made: that the goodness of God might be manifested on the one hand and his severity on the other. What man would be wise if he initiated something for an end that he knew he would not attain? God knows all things in advance; he knows that the wicked will be condemned. Therefore, we will not say that he makes unto salvation those who are to be condemned.

There was another argument: If God wills an end, he also wills the means to that end. I admit this: he wills the endurance of the martyrs; therefore, he wills persecutions. He does will them, but not in the same way. That which is good, he wills through itself. The persecutions that are carried out by tyrants he wills in a certain way, that is, for the sake of something else. He wills to tolerate, to not prevent; he wills to use those things. And when I say *in a certain way*, one ought not to infer: therefore, in a manner of speaking; falsely. John says [1 John 3:9], "He who has been born of God does not sin"—meaning, against the Holy Spirit and without repentance. From the fact that he does not sin in a certain sense, one may not infer that he sins in a manner of speaking, because this does not follow; for he sins truly, not in a manner of speaking and falsely. Likewise the law is holy in and of itself [Rom. 7:12], but in a certain sense it is the cause of anger and condemnation—yet not falsely; not in a manner of speaking. For Paul speaks this way [Rom. 4:15], and he speaks truly.

Therefore, the inference does not follow: "God wills in a certain way; therefore, he wills that thing falsely and

---

16. Zwingli, *Sermonis de providentia Dei anamnema* 6 ("A Sermon on the Providence of God," 183).

in a manner of speaking. For if God wills those things that contribute to an end, and wills sins in a certain way, because he has decreed not to prevent them and wills to use them, and if his will is immutable, then there will be iron-clad necessity." I reply: there will be necessity, but not compulsion. And if our will be deserted by God's grace, it is in the necessity of sinning. But God's providence, as far as his own decrees are concerned, is iron-clad and unbending. For Zechariah says of the chariots and empires that were going to succeed him, "They were going through iron mountains" [Zech. 6:1]. God's decrees are absolutely firm. And Christ says, "No one can snatch out of my hand those whom the Father has given me" [John 10:28–29].

But there seems to be an impediment to this opinion. In Psalm 68 [69:28] we read, "Let them be blotted out from the book of the living." Therefore, it seems his will is not unchanging, if those who had previously been written are blotted out. Read Augustine on this passage: "A man says, 'What I have written I have written;' and will God blot out what he has written? How then are they said to be blotted out? This expression is according to their expectation: they were not truly written, but thought they had been written."[17]

But there are those who attribute blindings and hardenings only to foreknowledge. On the contrary, it is not bare foreknowledge of those events, but a certain will of God, by which God is able to foreknow only those future things which are going to take place. And things which shall be, or which are, are not able to be, now or in the

---

17. Augustine, *Enarrationes in Psalmos* 68.13 (*Expositions on the Psalms* 69.29, *NPNF* 1/8:310).

future, unless by some kind of will God wills for them to be or to happen. Thus, a certain will of God precedes foreknowledge: he wills to not prevent; he wills to use them for his predestined plans.

33. Another argument: Those tyrants, Nebuchadnezzar, Sennacherib, and the rest, were like a staff and a rod in God's hand; therefore, God seems to have been the cause of sin. They were like a rod, this is certain; and afterward they were hurled into the fire once they had performed their function. Yet they were not senseless, but were moved by their own evil will, and so they are justly punished. For there are two kinds of instruments, as I explained above. And this is not a fraud—that God wills to make use of those evils and also issues orders against committing them. Those men commit the evils out of evil will; God makes use of their wickedness. Human beings too can use the evil actions of their enemies in a good way, and they often do so without any fraud; that is, with the intention of taking precautions for themselves and displaying endurance. God uses sins to punish sinners themselves sometimes—or rather, always, because sin is always a punishment of the sinner—and sometimes to punish others.

Another argument was that God put it into David's heart to number the people [2 Sam. 24:1]. Scripture does indeed speak in this way. We hear those expressions not in the poets but in the word of God. Plato was able to expel the poets from his Republic;[18] we are not able to eject the Scriptures that speak like this. But I have shown above how these statements ought to be understood. God withdrew his help; he did not hinder David; he willed to use

---

18. Plato, *Republic* 10.595a–608b.

that deed in order to punish the people. But the objection is raised: If God withdraws grace, he does so justly. I admit it—yet he does withdraw it. Moreover, he uses even the devil. In Chronicles [1 Chr. 21:1] it is said that the devil impelled David; therefore, God acted as well, because he permitted this to the devil.

But they object against that which we have often stated: that once grace has been withdrawn, sin creeps in of itself, since our will of itself inclines to this—just as in nature, once light has been withdrawn, darkness follows. God, they say, is like the sun, because its light is everywhere, but there are people who turn away into corners. But if his illumination is everywhere, what corners could people go into where that light would not be? The divine Scripture speaks otherwise, for it says of that man who misused his talent, "Take it away from him" [Matt. 25:28]. David prays, "Do not take away your Spirit from me" [Psalm 51:11]. Therefore, God willed to use David's sin in order to punish the people. And the accusation is unjust which some people level against the tragedian Aeschylus for saying that if God wills to ruin and destroy certain people, he supplies causes and occasions.[19] After all, this is how Scripture speaks, which can speak against the laws of Plato but not against the laws of God. For it says that the sons of Eli did not listen to their father because God willed to destroy them [1 Sam. 2:25], and that Rehoboam did not listen to the elders because the turning away was from God [1 Kings 12:15].

---

19. This fragment of Aeschylus is quoted by Plato in *Republic* 2.380a2–3 but not otherwise attested: θεὸς μὲν αἰτίαν φύει βροτοῖς, / ὅταν κακῶσαι δῶμα παμπήδην θέλῃ.

It was said: If this were how things stand, then God would not be the cause of all things, if he were not the cause of sins. This does not follow. For even though God is not the cause of sin, still he governs the sins that are committed, he uses them, and he makes the very groundwork, insofar as it is a physical thing. "But sin ought to be voluntary." If we are speaking of actual sin, it is true, but it is not true of original sin. Also the first motions, which are sins, are not voluntary. And Bernard in *On Free Choice* posits degrees of human nature.[20] Those who are beatified in the heavenly land are not able to sin; Adam was able not to sin; we, after sin, are not able not to sin. This is the case with the damned, with the reprobate and wicked. But the upright and the regenerate are able not to yield to sin, and to ensure that it does not hold complete sway, and they have this capacity from the Spirit of God. Hence it appears from that division that the sin of the damned is necessary, even though it is still sin. For although it is a necessary thing, it is still voluntary, but not voluntary in such a way that we are capable of ourselves to choose the other option, the one that is its contrary. For we cannot have a choice of the other option except from the same Spirit of God. Sins are punished justly, but regard is paid not to what you are capable or incapable of but to whether what you are doing is contrary to God's law. And God does not do injustice to anyone. Hence, that objection is not valid as far as God is concerned.

It seems like cruelty if someone fails to extend a hand to a blind man when he sees him lose his footing, or if

---

20. Bernard of Clairvaux, *De gratia et libero arbitrio* 7.21–8.26 (*On Grace and Free Choice*, 78–83).

he fails to help him up. God sees that a man will fall; he does not extend a hand; it seems like cruelty. In whom? In men, because it is for them that the law has been prescribed. God is not subject to those laws. This is Zwingli's response in his book *On Providence* and in his book *On False and True Religion*, where he is dealing with merit.[21] But even if God does not give as much to the reprobate as he does to others, still he does give them many things.[22] The preaching of the gospel is presented to them; he grants them many other things, even though he does not take pity on them unto salvation. God can do what he wills with what is his own.

You say: Those men reject mercy. Jerome, *On Jonah*: "God is merciful and kind by nature, prepared to save by mercy those whom he cannot save by justice; but we cast aside the mercy he offers."[23] I admit it, insofar as mercy is offered by general preaching. Yet God does not change their wills, and who denies that he could do this? If he does not will, he justly does not will. Augustine in *On the Good of Perseverance*, chapter 4: "In the same matter we see diverse judgments of God, and in diverse matters a single judgment."[24] There were twins in Rebecca's womb;

---

21. Zwingli, *Sermonis de providentia Dei anamnema* 4 ("A Sermon on the Providence of God," 169–70); *De vera et falsa religione* 24 (*On True and False Religion*, 272).

22. *multa* Samuel 1564: *multaque* London 1576: *multa quoque* Zurich 1580, Heidelberg 1603.

23. Jerome, *Commentarii in Ionam prophetam* 3.9 (*PL* 25:1137).

24. Augustine, *De dono perseverantiae* 8.17 (*On the Gift of Perseverance*, *NPNF* 1/5:531).

even before they had done anything good or bad, it was said, "Jacob I loved, but Esau I hated" [Mal. 1:2–3]. In the vineyard some men worked for the whole day, others for only one hour, yet they receive the same wage [Matt. 20:1–15].

As for the case of the household head whose sons or slaves sin, and he says, "I did not urge them on," the household head is justly accused, because he has a law prescribed. But God does not have a law prescribed for himself. He prescribes for his own self that he not do anything unjustly, but his will is the first yardstick of justice. God deserts the reprobate and is deserted by them, and he acts rightly. The fact that he deserts those who desert him is attested in 2 Chronicles 25 [v. 7]. Azariah, the son of Obed the prophet, says to king Amasa, "When you abandon him, he himself will abandon you" [2 Chr. 15:2]. God is present everywhere through his essence and power; he is present in his own people through his favor, grace, and help. In the first two of these modes he does not desert the wicked, but he does in the third.

Anselm's opinion was brought forward, from *On the Fall of the Devil*: "If God creates a son through a shameful action like adultery, why can he not will to create a son—insofar as this is a physical thing—through an evil will?"[25] We grant that the subject is created by God, but we need to take into consideration the defect that is in him afterward.

---

25. Anselm, *De casu diaboli* 20 (*PL* 158:352).

[CHAPTER 13:
IN WHAT SENSE THE WILL IS FREE]

34. In Acts we read that they came together against Christ to do what God's hand and counsel had decreed [4:28], and that Christ was handed over by the definite counsel of God [2:23]. In the case of Christ's death, the divine will is differently disposed as concerns Christ and as concerns the Jews. As far as Christ is concerned, God willed that he endure the cross out of obedience and out of charity, because he is our redemption; the divine nature brought about in him the ability to endure it. As for the Jews acting so savagely, God permitted this, but in that permission was a will to not hinder their evil will, so that he might make use of it and redemption might ensue. He could have hindered it if he had so willed, as is clear from what Jesus says: "Could the Father not give me eleven legions of angels to fight on my behalf?" [Matt. 26:53]. He used that sin in order to redeem us. Many things were suggested by God to the Jews which were good, such as preaching, miracles, and rebukes which he applied, but because of their vice they were swept along in an evil direction. Thus they were left in the necessity of sinning.

Where will free choice be? It has been lost. Augustine in chapter 30 in his *Manual for Laurentius*: "When man sinned, he lost himself and his free choice."[1] He says this twice in this chapter and elsewhere as well. It is also taught in book 2 of the *Sentences*, distinction 25.[2] But Bernard says that it was not lost.[3] These authorities are not at odds with each other if they be rightly understood. For Augustine takes free choice as the free faculty of choosing opposite things, this one or that. Now while we are unregenerated, we are not able to do things that are truly pleasing to God unless we be renewed through the Son of God, because free choice does not remain in us as far as those things are concerned. When Bernard says that it remains, what does he mean? Although they sin, they are not forced; they have consent, they exercise will: free choice of this kind remains.

Bernard clarifies himself when he posits a threefold freedom.[4] The will has freedom from compulsion; freedom from sin, once it has been regenerated; and freedom from misery, when it will be in the heavenly land. We do not have freedom from misery in this present world; we do have freedom from necessity. By necessity he means coercion. This is clear from Bernard, for he posits freedom of choice in God: he is good of necessity, yet this does not do away with his freedom. The angels and saints in the heavenly land are not able to sin, yet they have free will.

---

1. Augustine, *Enchiridion* 30 (*Enchiridion*, NPNF 1/3:247).

2. Peter Lombard, *Sententiae* 2.25.7 (*Sentences*, 2:119).

3. Bernard, *De gratia et libero arbitrio* 8.24 (*On Grace and Free Choice*, 80–81).

4. Bernard, *De gratia et libero arbitrio* 3.6–8 (*On Grace and Free Choice*, 61–64).

He even gives freedom to the devil and to the damned: although they are not able to be good, yet the evil which they will, they will of their own accord, not because they are capable of the contrary.

Again, he says, "It is grace that preserves, it is choice that is preserved."[5] How so? It acquires soundness; that is, it assents, it consents. But he does not say that it consents of itself. On the contrary, he brings forward the passage of Paul: "For we are not able to think anything good of ourselves" [2 Cor. 3:5], much less to consent, and: "God works in us to will and to perform" [Phil. 2:13]. He says that God proposes good thoughts without us by going ahead of us. Afterward, he says, God changes the will, changes the affection, so that with the will changed, consent may follow. Hence he says that God does four things in us. First, he rouses, by introducing good thoughts; secondly, he heals, that is, changes the will; thirdly, he strengthens, that is, leads to act; fourthly, he preserves, so that we do not feel a defect, so that we persevere, so that a good action is brought to completion.

---

5. Bernard, *De gratia et libero arbitrio* 14.46–47 (*On Grace and Free Choice*, 105–6).

[CHAPTER 14: IN WHAT SENSE SIN IS PART OF GOD'S WILL]

35. In brief, we too assert that, as far as sin is concerned, God is "*not responsible* for all evils" [ἀναίτιον πάντων κακῶν], as Epiphanius writes,[1] because he is not properly the cause; nevertheless, he is not asleep. Secondly, that term also has the meaning of *unblameable*. God cannot be dragged into court by us: he does justly whatever he does. For our part, we add that it is a universal belief, and one that must be maintained in the Church, that nothing either good or evil happens in the world without the providence of God. Human actions are not able to overstep God's providence: "Because all the hairs of our head are numbered" [Matt. 10:29]. If sparrows, the most paltry little birds, do not fall to the ground without the will of God, what shall we say of human actions, which are far more excellent? Divine providence has the very widest scope. Even though it does not operate in the same way with good things and with evil ones, still they do not happen apart from God's providence, which is the divine will by which things are

---

1. Epiphanius, *Adversus haereses* 64.28.6 (*Panarion*, 160).

governed powerfully and in the most excellent way and are directed to their proper ends.

Nor should we be offended that he leaves certain evils in the world. For even though they are adverse to individual natures, still they contribute to the common good. If all evils had been taken away, we would lack many benefits. Hence the saying that there would be no lion life were it not for the slaughters of the sheep that lions eat, and the endurance of the martyrs would not exist if the cruelty of tyrants were not permitted by God.

It seems that an impediment is posed to this belief of ours by what Plato says in book 2 of *On the Republic*: that God is the author of few things for human beings, because there are many evils among human beings and God is not the cause of any evils.[2] Hence he seems to confine God's providence within narrow limits. If he means the efficient cause, and is talking about sins, we grant it; yet in the meantime providence is not snoring. However, in this passage Plato teaches something that absolutely should not be granted by the upright, because he denies that the gods come to human beings in the likeness of strangers. But angels were received as guests by Abraham and Lot. His statement that God cannot change with respect to his substance is true, but we must grant that God sometimes appeared[3] in other forms. With Moses he spoke out of the

---

2. Plato, *Republic* 2.379c2–4.

3. *quod non in aliquibus ... apparuerit, non est* Samuel 1564: *quod in aliquibus ... apparuerit non est* London 1576: *quod in aliquibus ... apparuerit, est* Zurich 1580, Heidelberg 1603. The awkward double negative in Samuel 1564 caused trouble in the transmission of this passage. London 1576 omitted the first *non*, thus reversing the proper

burning bush; on Mount Sinai he made himself known by words; he showed himself to the prophets under various appearances. I think that Plato is talking about those repulsive transformations by which the poets say he was transformed into a swan, an eagle, or a bull. Such things must be banished from God.

36. But my assertion that all things whatsoever are directed by God's providence, and that what Plato says does not pose a hindrance, does not seem sufficient. For [John] Damascene also sets himself in opposition to it. In book 2, chapter 29,[4] he says that τὰ οὐκ ἐφ' ἡμῖν—"those things that do not depend on us"—are subject to God's providence, for he adds: τὰ γὰρ ἐφ' ἡμῖν, οὐκ τῆς προνοίας ἐστι, ἀλλὰ τοῦ ἡμετέρου αὐτεξουσίου, "Those things that depend on us do not belong to God's providence but to our free will."[5] Are then those actions of ours which he says depend on us not in the providence of God? Let they who are so inclined believe this: *I* do not believe it. He adds something even harsher: ἡ μὲν αἵρεσις τῶν πρακτῶν ἐφ' ἡμῖν ἐστί, τὸ δὲ τέλος τῶν ἀγαθῶν τῆς τοῦ θεοῦ συνεργείας, "The choice of doing things rests with us, but the fulfillment and completion of good things depends on God's cooperation." Who will say this—that if we choose to do the things that are good, it comes from us? The apostle says, "God works in us to will and to perform" [Phil. 2:13]. But when Damascene

---

meaning of the sentence; subsequent editions removed both occurrences of *non*, and so restored the correct meaning.

4. John of Damascus, *The Fount of Knowledge* 2.29 (*Writings*, 261).

5. Here, and again a few sentences below, Vermigli inserts the Greek text of Damascene followed by his own Latin translation.

withdraws those things from divine providence, I do not approve.

He divides providence into εὐδοκία, *good pleasure*, and συγχώρησις, *permission*.[6] I am not opposed to these categories; I have laid down both of them: providence not only directs good things but also brings them about, whereas it permits evil things—but not in such a way that it leaves them entirely to themselves, for it uses them. But he makes a distinction within that permission [συγχώρησις] or abandonment [ἐγκατάληψις] and posits another sort that is directive [οἰκονομική] and instructive [παιδευτική], since it contributes to the instruction of the saints if they be left for a time. It is sometimes said to be τέλεια: *complete* and, so to speak, *past hope*, when people's vice makes them incorrigible and they perish.[7] We too affirm that God leaves his elect for a time; others he leaves permanently.

Next, he says that God *antecedently* [προηγουμένως] wills for people to become participants in salvation, but later on he wills to punish them when they sin. He calls this a *following will* [θέλημα ἑπόμενον], as though it follows from our vice.[8] For my part, I say that God's will is simple, but its objects are diverse. There are the elect whom he wills to be saved; there are also the reprobate whom he wills to be punished for their sins. But we should not stop there: he wills to manifest his power in them. Therefore, I affirm providence to be universal, Damascene posing no

---

6. John of Damascus, *The Fount of Knowledge* 2.29 (*Writings*, 261).

7. John of Damascus, *The Fount of Knowledge* 2.29 (*Writings*, 262).

8. John of Damascus, *The Fount of Knowledge* 2.29 (*Writings*, 262–63).

impediment. This is what Augustine also thought, sentence 58: "Nothing is done visibly or perceptibly which is not ordered or permitted from the invisible or intelligible court of the highest Commander;" and so he exempts nothing from divine providence.[9]

37. These are the things which I judged necessary to say about this topic. There could be many more besides, but I must impose a limit. I do know that Philip Melanchthon, that venerable man, whom I love and accept, seems to say something different; but here I appeal to the very same man in his old *Common Places*. Read what he has to say about predestination and free choice. He says (something that I perhaps would not have said) that the term *free choice* is completely foreign to the divine writings and to the judgment and meaning of the Spirit. He says that Platonic philosophy has weakened the piety of the Church from the beginning.[10] At the conclusion of this passage, he says, "To come now to our inward and outward acts: if they be referred to providence, all things happen as they have been ordained. But in outward actions, if they be referred to the will, there is freedom there." If we consider the inward good things that God requires, he says there is not freedom there; if the affections begin to rage, they cannot be restrained.[11] Ambrose says the same thing

---

9. Augustine, *De trinitate* 3.4.9 (*On the Trinity*, *NPNF* 1/3:59).

10. Philip Melanchthon, *Loci communes rerum theologicarum* (Mainz: Johann Schöffer, 1522), p. 9 (*Loci Communes*, 70–72).

11. Melanchthon, *Loci communes rerum theologicarum*, p. 19 (*Loci Communes*, 81).

in *On Luke*,[12] and Augustine often quotes him as saying that our heart is not in our own power.[13] Others do not disagree with them: Zwingli and Luther, those heroes of the Reformed faith; Oecolampadius, Bucer, Calvin. I can bring forward other authors too, but I do not operate by counting votes.

I have said that God, properly speaking, is not the cause of sin, and that nothing happens in the world, whether good or bad, apart from the providence of God. But if I have failed to reach my goal, it grieves me. If someone shows by adequate evidence that this opinion is impious or harmful to good morals, I am prepared to change. But I have addressed this topic at greater length because it is a matter of enormous importance and one that recurs often in the sacred writings. And things that are set forth cohesively are better understood than those that are set forth piecemeal here and there.

---

12. Ambrose, *Expositio evangelii secundum Lucam* 2.3.84 (*PL* 15:1583).

13. Augustine, *De dono perseverantiae* 8.19–20 (*On the Gift of Perseverance*, *NPNF* 1/5:532); *Contra duas epistulas Pelagianorum* 4.11.30 (*Against Two Letters of the Pelagians*, *NPNF* 1/5:431–32).

[CHAPTER 15: GOD'S TWOFOLD WILL]

[We have added these few things from a similar discussion on 1 Samuel chapter 2.]

38. Now it remains for us to speak[1] about the will of God itself. First, then, I confess that I am not displeased with that distinction which the scholastics customarily use when they postulate that there is one *will of the sign* and another *efficacious will* or, as some of them write, *will of good pleasure.*[2]

The will of the sign is that which indicates what we ought to do and what we ought to avoid. For from it we infer God's judgment and ordinance. It consists in the law, commands, promises, threats, and counsels. So it is

---

1. *dicamus* Samuel 1564, London 1576, Zurich 1580: *fusius dicamus* Heidelberg 1603.

2. In Latin, *voluntas signi* and *voluntas beneplaciti*. This famous distinction originated with Hugh of St. Victor. It was adopted by Peter Lombard, Alexander of Hales, and Bonaventure, among other scholastic writers, and became a commonplace of Protestant scholastic theology. For discussion, see Muller, *Post-Reformation Reformed Dogmatics*, 3:456–59.

to this type of will that the statement we cited above is applicable: "You are not a God who wills iniquity;" and also this one: "You have hated falsehood and iniquity" [Psalm 5:4–6], plus all those testimonies from which it can be shown that God does not will sins. And indeed how can he will them, when he has issued a law against them? when he punishes them with the utmost severity? when he has implanted abhorrence of sins in the minds of upright people? when he has allowed his most beloved Son to be driven to the cross for the purpose of taking away sin? However, we should note that many things are committed and done contrary to this will of God which is called the will of the sign. Indeed, there are a great number of wicked men who turn away from the law of God, harass his preachers, slay his prophets, even formerly killed the Son of God himself. And we should not omit the fact that this is truly called and truly is the will of God, since Christ says, "He who does the will of my Father, this one is my mother and my brother and my sister" [Matt. 12:50]. And in Deuteronomy it is written, "What else does God will than that you love him and walk in his ways?" [10:12].

Besides this, there is the other will of God which is called powerful, efficacious, and the will of good pleasure. It cannot be overcome and vanquished by any power, since it is written of it, "He has done all things whatever he has willed" [Psalm 115:3]. And Paul says of it, "Who can resist his will?" [Rom. 9:19]. And assuredly if something could happen when God is unwilling and not consenting, this will would be weak and feeble.

Now these twin wills are not so distinct as though they were two things or two faculties located in God, since that act turns out to be absolutely simple. But since God does not always disclose his counsel to people in its full scope and entirety (for this is not necessary, since he has sufficiently revealed that which suffices for obtaining salvation), as a result of this there is a difference between those two wills of his. For that which he has revealed in some way is to be referred to the will of the sign, while that which he has reserved for himself alone as secret and private belongs to the will of good pleasure.

But we should illustrate this by excellent and plain examples, so that it may be more easily understood. God ordered Abraham to go sacrifice Isaac, his only begotten son [Gen. 22:1–2]. In this precept, undoubtedly, the will of the sign was contained. For God revealed to Abraham only that he willed to put his obedience to the test, and did not indicate that he willed to later prevent Isaac's being sacrificed. Obviously this prevention followed later on, and the will of good pleasure was not disclosed earlier. Thus we can establish that the will of good pleasure and the will of the sign is one and the same, but it is called by different names depending on whether it was known to us or unknown. Again, it was said to Hezekiah, "Put your house in order, for you are going to die soon" [2 Kings 20:1]. Certainly considering the virulence of the disease and the order of nature, the king was absolutely going to die, and his death was God's will insofar as it could be inferred from a natural sign and from the prophet's words. Yet because God of his own mercy had decided to prolong his life for many years in view of his repentance[3] and tears, this will of his was both an effica-

---

3. *poenitentiae* Samuel 1564, Zurich 1580, Heidelberg 1603: *potenti-*

cious will and a will of good pleasure. Again, by the will of the sign the Ninevites are threatened with destruction after forty days, even though God by his will of good pleasure has determined to forgive them upon their repentance [Jonah 3]. This will is connected with the other one, for those who fall away from the other one run up against this one, and those who despise that will of God by which he offers the law, promises, threats, and counsels rush into the one by which sinners pay the penalty for their wicked deeds.

39. For this reason Augustine in his *Manual for Laurentius*, chapter 101, very elegantly says, "What God wills is certainly either from us or about us. From us, when we live rightly; about us, when we pay the penalty for the sins we have committed."[4] And in chapter 102 he says, "Sinners act contrary to God's law as far as lies in them; but as far as his omnipotence is concerned, they cannot so act."[5] In fact Gregory too in his *Moralia*, chapter 11, book 6, wrote, "Many people carry out the will of God when they strain every nerve to alter it, and by resisting they unwittingly comply with the divine plan."[6] Joseph also expressed this opinion in his answer to his brothers: "You indeed sold me, but it was God's plan to send me into Egypt ahead of you so I might prepare both food and deliverance for you" [Gen. 45:4–7]. Therefore,

---

ae London 1576.

4. Augustine, *Enchiridion* 101 (*Enchiridion, NPNF* 1/3:270); Vermigli paraphrases here.

5. Augustine, *Enchiridion* 102 (*Enchiridion, NPNF* 1/3:270).

6. Gregory, *Moralia in Iob* 6.18.28 (*PL* 75:745).

it is this will by which God predestines the elect to eternal life. It is obscure to us and yet, being most powerful, it cannot be weakened.

From this distinction in the divine will, we sufficiently understand how we should respond when we are faced with the objection that God made man to be a living soul and, therefore, does not will for him to perish. For we affirm that this is true as far as the will of the sign is concerned, since he gave man the law, promises, threats, and counsels, and if man had embraced these things, he would certainly have lived. But if we look to that other will which is powerful and efficacious, it certainly cannot be denied in the least that he willed for man to die. For as we learn in chapter 16 [v. 4] of Proverbs, "God has created all things for his own sake, even the wicked man for the evil day." And Paul teaches that God, like a potter, fashions some vessels indeed for glory but others for disgrace [Rom. 9:21–23]. It is also this will by which God rules, governs, and moderates people's depraved lusts and sins, as was said, in keeping with his own choice. By this will God hands over the wicked to a reprobate mind, sends in the Chaldeans to lead away his people captive, adds effectiveness to illusions, wills for the wicked to be led astray, and is said to harden them.

40. But since these things are distinctly read and they turn up frequently in the sacred writings, we must attentively consider how they should be taken. The common crowd supposes that when it is written that God blinds, hardens, hands over, sends in, or deceives, this means nothing else than that he permits those things to happen. Many of the Fathers interpret those expressions along these lines, no doubt induced by the following

reason: they judged it to be wicked and blasphemous if God were considered to be the author of sin, and they did not want people to transfer the causes of their own sins to God himself. I strongly approve this intention of theirs, and I join them in admitting that such things happen by God's permission. For since he is able to prevent sins from happening and yet does not hinder them, he is rightly said to permit them. Hence Augustine in his *Manual for Laurentius*, chapter 98, rightly says that no mind is so depraved that God is not able to correct it if only he wills to do so, but to not prevent, when you are able, is the same as to permit.[7] The same author in *Against Julian*, book 5, chapter 3, teaches that there are many evils which God would certainly not permit if he did not will them.[8]

Nevertheless, we should also adduce something other than permission if we wish to do proper justice to the passages of Scripture which are raised in objection. For those who say that God merely permits sins are not able to exclude his will entirely, since he permits them either willingly or unwillingly. He obviously does not permit them unwillingly, because no one can force him; therefore, it follows that he willingly allows them to happen. We may not idly fancy that this will of permission is remiss in God, because there is nothing in God that is not perfect and complete. Therefore, we must posit that God not only permits but also, in some fixed way, wills

---

7. Augustine, *Enchiridion* 98 (*Enchiridion*, NPNF 1/3:268).

8. Augustine, *Contra Iulianum Pelagianum* 5.4.14 (*Against Julian the Pelagian*, 256).

sin—yet not insofar as it is sin, seeing that of necessity his will always inclines toward the good, but insofar as it is a punishment for earlier deeds of wickedness. For in this respect, even though it is sin, it still takes on the form of good.[9]

In the same way, princes and magistrates sometimes unleash lions and wild beasts upon evildoers and goad elephants against their enemies. They themselves did not make these kinds of beasts, but still they utilize their savageness and ferocity. So God employs the work of tyrants when he wills to exact just punishment from some people. Hence the king of Babylon is called a hammer, a staff, and the saw of the Lord's hand, since God willed through his violence to chasten the Israelite people [Jer. 51:20]. For that king, exceedingly powerful though he was, was not capable of afflicting the Jews by his own strength. On the contrary, he is censured for his arrogance because he sometimes ascribed this to his own might. For God testifies that he himself is the real author of such great destruction.

And Job, when he had been grievously tormented by the Sabeans and Chaldeans and also by the devil, and had been cut off from almost all his possessions, said with no less uprightness than wisdom, "The Lord gave,[10] the Lord has taken away" [Job 1:21]. And in order to show more clearly that this had happened by the will of God, he added, "As it pleased God, so it happened."

---

9. *subit* Samuel 1564, Zurich 1580, Heidelberg 1603: *subdit* London 1576.

10. *Dominus dedit* Samuel 1564, London 1576: *om.* Zurich 1580, Heidelberg 1603.

For he saw that God had utilized the Chaldeans and Sabeans and the devil as instruments. And in the second book of Samuel, chapter 24 [v. 1], we are told that God stirred David up to make a census of the people, but in Chronicles this deed is attributed to the devil [1 Chr. 21:1]. Now both of these things were true, because God incited him to do this through the instrumentality and operation of the devil. For as Solomon says, "The king's heart is in the hand of God, and God inclines it wherever he has willed" [Prov. 21:1]—not, indeed, as has often been said already, by instilling a new wickedness, but by utilizing the wickedness that he finds, either to punish sins or to bring about other plans of his own. Therefore, when it is written that God hardens or that he blinds, we must believe that he not only abandons or deserts but also brings his own will to bear.

41. And we should not pass over the fact that in chapters 6 and 7 of Exodus [7:3] it is written that God hardened Pharaoh's heart, yet in chapter 8 [vv. 15, 32] it is written that Pharaoh himself made his own heart stubborn. Thus, both of these things are true. Indeed, Pharaoh first had the beginnings of such great stubbornness in himself, and opposed himself to God's word voluntarily and by his own will. But on the other hand, as we have shown above, God ensured that this hardness of his mind should be brought to light, and he moderated it and governed it according to his own choice. We should not imagine that God holds sway over the world in such a way that he sits in a watchtower like an idle man and does nothing there, nor that he gives loose reins to the world and to events down below as if to a horse, allowing them to wander wherever they please. Nor is it true what

some people claim, that God neither wills nor does not will the evils or sins themselves, as though he does not think about them at all—in the same way that if someone were to ask me whether I will for the king of Gaul to go hunting today, I could rightly respond that I neither will nor do not will this, since it is no concern of mine at all. But we cannot rightly make this response concerning God, since whatever happens in the nature of things is relevant to his care and providence.

But I should wish those people to consider from what testimony of Scripture they are capable of corroborating that *permission* of theirs which they cling to so tenaciously. I am not unaware that they bring forward in their favor what we read in Psalm 81 [v. 12]: "I permitted them to the desires of their heart." However, if one consults the Hebrew truth, it will appear that this evidence is weaker and feebler than they think. For the verb *schillach* in the Hebrew is in the Piel form, which by the force of the conjugation signifies a powerful action, and it is inappropriate for us to weaken it by translating it as *permission*. On the contrary, it agrees with the phrase of Paul by which it is said in the letter to the Romans that God handed over the wicked to a reprobate mind [1:28]. God is shown to have cast the wicked away rather than permitted them. But to where has he permitted them or cast them away? Why, into their own depraved desires; that is, to be wholly possessed and ruled by them.

And that Hebrew verb is frequently employed with this meaning in the sacred writings. For in Genesis we learn that God cast out humans from paradise [3:23]. Who would translate the verb *cast out* there as *permitted*? On the contrary, he ejected and dislodged humans from there. Then again, in chapter 19 [v. 13] the angels say, "And God sent us to destroy Sodom." In this passage, *send forth* cannot be equivalent to *permit*. And in Ezekiel it is written, "It sent forth a shoot" [17:6], even though a vine does not *permit* a shoot to go out from it but rather *drives* it to go forth. Therefore, let the interpreter ponder how in this passage he can possibly render the Hebrew verb *schillach* by the verb *permit*.

42. And we should not omit the fact that the divine writings ascribe God's permission no less to good things than to evil ones. For in the letter to the Hebrews, chapter 6 [v. 3], when he is talking about good things, the apostle says, "If God permits." Julian the Pelagian (as appears from Augustine's treatise against him, book 5, chapter 3) was of the opinion that when God is said in the Scriptures to *hand over* or to *blind*, we should take it to mean merely that he *abandons* or *permits*. But Augustine on the contrary says that God not only permits but, as the apostle taught, manifests his own wrath and power.[11] Moreover, Julian teaches that such expressions are hyperbolic, whereas Augustine contends that they have their proper meaning. Julian interprets that those who are said to have been handed over to their own desires had been afflicted by those diseases previously, and so he adds, "Why did they need to be handed over to them? It was enough that they be allowed to wallow and rest in the same desires." To this Augustine says, "Do you think that to have desires is the same as to be handed over to them? For the wicked are handed over to evil lusts not

---

11. Augustine, *Contra Iulianum Pelagianum* 5.3.13 (*Against Julian the Pelagian*, 254–55).

only so that they have them but so that they are entirely held fast and possessed by them." Therefore, the same Father added, "Just as God acts in the bodies of the wicked by troubling and afflicting them, so also he operates in their minds by impelling them into sins."[12] And in the same place he discusses the history of Shimei, where David says, "The Lord has ordered him to curse me" [2 Sam. 16:11]. Augustine says, "The Lord justly inclined the will of Shimei, which was evil because of his own vice, so that he attacked David with abusive insults, and the cause is stated: 'Surely the Lord will repay me with good things in return for this curse' [2 Sam. 16:12]."[13] The same Augustine also writes in *On Grace and Free Choice* that God operates in people's minds, inclining them to both good things and to evil ones by a judgment that is often hidden, sometimes manifest, but always just.[14]

To this you may add: It is extremely difficult to explain how and for what reason God does these things. However, we must lay it down as absolutely certain that these evils, insofar as they proceed from God, are not sins but right and good things, but insofar as they come from the devil or from human beings, they should rightly be accounted as sins. The Manichees, because they could not extricate themselves from this problem, fancied that there are two fundamental principles in things, one of

---

12. Augustine, *Contra Iulianum Pelagianum* 5.3.11 (*Against Julian the Pelagian*, 252–53).

13. Augustine, *De gratia et libero arbitrio* 20.41 (*On Grace and Free Choice*, 177).

14. Augustine, *De gratia et libero arbitrio* 21.43 (*On Grace and Free Choice*, 180–81).

which is good and the other evil. We, on the other hand, teach that the one God is the author of all good things, but we say that sins arose out of Adam's defection from God—yet that they are tempered and ruled by God's will and choice. Hence, we conclude that the actions themselves, that is, the subjects of sins, are from God, and that he himself withdraws his grace and help when it seems good to him. Moreover, he rules and bends people's depraved lusts wherever it pleases him. And since he utilizes people's sins for the punishments of other sins, it cannot be said that he did not will them in any way.

With Adam's sin, however, the issue is more difficult, because there had not been any preceding fall of his for God to be punishing by a later sin. But to this we reply that his action—that is, the subject of the deformity and injustice—was from God, whereas the privation or defect was from the free choice of Adam, whom God had created whole, free, and complete, yet not in such a way that he could not fall away and wander off. And the grace of God by which he was being kept from falling was not so great as to establish him securely. Yet there can be no doubt that God willed for Adam to fall; otherwise, he would not have fallen. But he willed him to fall not indeed in respect of sin, but so he might use this fall to disclose the wealth and immense riches of his goodness, and might show that he was able not only to render man whole and perfect but also restore him once he was fallen and lost. And for this reason he sent his own Son to die on the cross for the human race. This is why Gregory exclaimed, "O fortunate fault that deserved to have such a redeemer!"[15]

---

15. In Latin, *O felix culpa, quae talem meruit habere Redemptorem*—a famous line that was often attributed to Gregory the Great. A similar sentiment can be found in Gregory's commentary *In I Librum Regum* 4.10 (8.7): *Nam quae maior culpa, quam illa, per quam omnes morimur? Et quae maior bonitas, quam illa, per quam a morte omnes liberamur? Et quidem, nisi Adam peccaret, redemptorem nostrum ex virgine carnem nostram suscipere non oporteret* (*Corpus Christianorum Series Latina* 144:301). However, the quotation also replicates almost verbatim a line from the hymn *Exultet*: *O felix culpa quae talem et tantum meruit habere redemptorem.*

[CHAPTER 16: CONFORMING OURSELVES TO GOD'S WILL]

43. But we must carefully note this point: that God sometimes approves these things even though he is not pleased that they happen. This is not because there are two wills in him, for he has only one will, although this will has diverse objects. For he considers our mind and counsel, which often is approved by him. But on the other hand, he has the plan of his own providence before his eyes, which he wills to be intact and stable in all ways. Therefore, he sometimes inspires in our hearts things that would be good by their own nature, yet he does not will for them to be brought to conclusion, because[1] they do not at all further the plan of his providence. In this way we say that Christ's prayer in which he prays to avoid death was pleasing to God [Matt. 26:39], even though he willed not to fulfill it. Christ did not will what he was asking for with a depraved or corrupted will but with a right and good one. However, the providence and predestination of God remained unmoved, by which he had determined that Christ should

---

1. *quod ad* Kings 1566, Zurich 1580, Heidelberg 1603: *quoad* London 1576.

be nailed to the cross at that time for our salvation. So we ought to purpose many things in a conscientious and upright fashion; but when we recognize that God wills for these things not to happen, we should shift our purposes over to his will.

But in order that I may treat this topic with greater clarity, before all else let us establish that human will must be conformed to the will of God in some way; otherwise, it would not be right, for that which is right must agree with God's rule. Yet it is not necessary that what God wills to happen be pleasing to us in all ways, for it is sometimes necessary that what he wills be displeasing to us—but rightly so and without sin. I will illustrate this point with examples so that it may be better understood. Moses heard that God willed to wipe out the people; he himself willed otherwise and was deeply grieved and interposed himself with pleas that this should not happen [Ex. 32:7–14]. Samuel likewise realized that Saul had been rejected, but he did not immediately acquiesce in this will of God; rather, he was grieved at the downfall of this king and wept for a long time on this account [1 Sam. 15:35]. Jeremiah, too, understood that Jerusalem was going to be overthrown, and he lamented this fall with many tears [Jer. 9:1–10].

Here some people say that God's decree or good pleasure is either known to us or unknown. Once it has been ascertained by us, we are bound to accommodate our will to it, but if it escapes our notice, we have the revealed law which we are able to follow safely. Now there is something in what these people say, but this opinion of theirs is not fully satisfactory. For Jeremiah and Christ were well aware that by God's decree and will the city of Jerusalem was absolutely going to be overthrown, and yet they wept on this account, and they did not sin in weeping. Moreover, it often happens that we learn God's will from his works themselves, even though we ought not to acquiesce in this will immediately. For instance, it sometimes happens that a son sees his father dying, and if he is a pious son, he realizes at the same time that God wills his death. But will he not grieve on this account, and will he not desire that his life be further prolonged?

What, then, should be done when such things occur? Certainly we will have to consider what accords with God's will and what accords with our own. Certainly it agrees with God's will that he act on the basis of his own goodness and justice, that he confer benefits on the good and punish the wicked. On the other hand, it accords with our will that it do things agreeable to itself. And what things agree with our nature we will discern from its constitution, that is, from the law of nature and of God, but sometimes also from an inward inspiration of the Spirit. And in this way we may be at variance with God's will in point of fact, even though we agree with it as far as the form and efficient cause are concerned. After all, God sometimes wills two things at the same time: namely, to punish the city, the race, and our parents, and for us to grieve on that account; and those things are not inconsistent with each other. God formerly willed for Sodom and Gomorrah to perish, and when he had disclosed this to Abraham, the latter was grieved in many ways and interceded for those who were going to perish [Gen. 18:23–32]. We are bound to believe that Abraham did not pour out those prayers apart from the inspiration of God's Spirit.

44. Yet another point must be added to these as well: the things which we realize that God wills can be con-

sidered in two ways. First, unqualifiedly and absolutely. In this respect we are bound to do the things that agree with our will or nature as rightly established. Alternatively, we will regard them with a rightful comparison to divine providence. If we compare them to that, it is necessary that we acquiesce in it absolutely. For as Augustine says in his *Manual*, it is wicked to struggle against divine providence.[2] To sum up, it is our part to will in all matters what God wills for us to will, and to do so with a right end, that is, with a good purpose, or (as people commonly put it) a right intention—even though, as far as the matter is concerned, that which seems good to God need not always be pleasing to us.

But if you ask what those things are which accord with our nature as well established, I reply: holy things, upright things, and just things. Hence, in the letter to the Philippians the apostle said, "Whatever things are true, upright, just, pure, fitting, of good report, if there is any praise, if any excellence, ponder these things and do them" [4:8]. For this reason, when David was resolving to build a temple, even though God willed that this not happen, still his will was approved as right and just [2 Sam. 7:1–13]. The holy king undoubtedly knew that God willed that a temple be built for him, and he had realized that this temple would be in Jerusalem. Thus his will was not devoid of piety. Moreover, since he was a son of God and was led by his Spirit, undoubtedly God was inspiring this will in him. We ought not always to consider what God is doing outwardly, but what he is doing within ourselves, and then we

---

2. This is not stated in so many words in the *Enchiridion*, but may be inferred from ch. 99–100 (*NPNF* 1/3:268–69).

ought to follow this. And he works in us both to will and to perform [Phil. 2:13]. Admittedly, he does not always work the perfection of the action, or a will that is perfect and whole. Nor are those two things always joined together, such that he works to will and to perform at the same time. For sometimes he brings about the willing only, and does not grant that the thing we will reaches effect.

And not only should our will be conformed to God's will, but also our understanding. For we should understand only those things that God has willed to disclose to us, and no further. Therefore, no one should say, "I will to understand the things that God himself knows." On these matters, there is a lucid treatment in the first distinction of the sentences, 48,[3] and in Augustine's *Manual*.[4]

---

3. Peter Lombard, *Sententiae* 1.48 (*Sentences*, 1:259–62).

4. Augustine, *Enchiridion* 101 (*Enchiridion*, NPNF 1/3:269–70). Heidelberg 1603 adds here, "See the theses on providence at the end of this work, after the topic of free choice." The theses in question may be found on p. 993 of that Heidelberg edition, under the title "On Providence and Predestination." "On Providence and Predestination" is one of three short tracts that were printed at the end of most printings of Vermigli's *Loci Communes* beginning with Rudolph Gualther's 1580 edition; the other two were entitled "On Free Choice" and "Whether God is the Cause and Author of Sin." Translations of all three can be found in McLelland, *Philosophical Works*, 320–34. Scholars have extensively debated the authorship of these three tracts, with some attributing them to Heinrich Bullinger and others affirming them to be Vermigli's handiwork. For a summary of the debate, see McLelland, *Philosophical Works*, 268–70, and Frank A. James III, "Confluence and Influence: Peter Martyr Vermigli and Thomas Aquinas on Predestination," in *Church and School in Early Modern Protestantism: Studies in Honor of Richard A. Muller on the Maturation of a Theological Tradition*, ed. Jordan Ballor, David Sytsma, and Jason Zuidema (Leiden: Brill, 2013), 169n.26.

PETER MARTYR VERMIGLI: FIRST PART OF THE COMMON PLACES

FIFTEENTH CHAPTER
In what sense God is said to repent and to tempt

[CHAPTER 1: WHAT IT MEANS FOR GOD TO REPENT]

1. Interpreters sweat a great deal about the sense in which repentance can be applicable to God. For God says, "I am God and I do not change" [Mal. 3:6]. And a little below,[1] "The triumpher of Israel does not change" [1 Sam. 15:29]. And Balaam says in the book of Numbers, "God is not like a man that he should change, nor like a son of man that he should lie" [23:19]. But in Genesis he says, "I repent that I have made man" [6:6]. Since these passages seem to be at odds, they must be reconciled.

    Some explain these passages in the following way. Just as the Holy Spirit is said to cry out and to make demands on our behalf with groans that cannot be uttered [Rom. 8:26], so God is said to perform repentance. The Spirit does not beseech, does not demand, does not groan, for he is God. But because he rouses us to beseeching, demanding, and groaning, he himself is said to do these very things. It is with this meaning that Paul orders us not

---

1. *infra* Samuel 1564, London 1576, Zurich 1580: *post* Heidelberg 1603.

to grieve the Spirit of God, that is, not to offend with our wicked deeds the saints in whom the Spirit of God dwells [Eph. 4:30]. In this way, because good men were grieved about Saul's wickedness and God had stirred up this feeling in them, God himself is said to be influenced by regret [1 Sam. 15:11]. Luther follows this explanation in his *On Genesis*.[2]

But Augustine in his *Book of Eighty-Three Questions*, question 52, where he treats this issue diligently, says that Scripture tends often to lower itself to our limited comprehension and to attribute to God things which we see happening in the ordinary experience of human life, since otherwise it could not be understood.[3] Thus, humans tend to take vengeance only when they are angry; consequently, the Scriptures say that God is angry when he takes vengeance. And men do not safeguard their wives' chastity without jealousy; consequently, because it is God's primary care that his Church, as his wife, may not consort with an adulterer, the Scriptures say that he is jealous. In this way feet and hands and other body parts are ascribed to God. In this way, too, because people tend to change their plan only if they repent of some action, the Scriptures say that God is influenced by regret whenever he changes his action. This is not because any change has taken place in God, but because there is a change in something that we hoped would last permanently. And it is with this mean-

---

2. Martin Luther, *Commentary on Genesis* 6.5–6 (*Lectures on Genesis*, 44).

3. Augustine, *De diversis quaestionibus octoginta tribus* 52 (*Eighty-Three Different Questions*, 88–89), from where the ensuing illustrations are drawn.

ing that God is said to have repented that he had made Saul king.

Others think that this issue can be resolved in an easier and simpler way if the change is understood to happen in the thing itself, not in God. To keep with the same example: previously Saul was pious and upright; now he has become wicked and rebellious; therefore, he seemed to deserve having God repent about him. This interpretation seems all the more probable because in the text itself[4] there follows, "And Saul departed" [1 Sam. 15:12].

2. The first opinion, even though it has some attractiveness, cannot be proved of all cases. Yes, God can be said to do that which he brings about in us, and he causes us to do it ourselves. But this does not square in every case. For he set fire to Sodom himself [Gen. 19:24]; he destroyed Pharaoh himself [Ex. 14:15–28]; and in so doing he indulged his own anger and vengeance, yet he did not impel people to do those things. And in this very passage,[5] although we read that God repented, no repentance is ascribed to Samuel. Augustine's opinion is simple and plausible. The third opinion too cannot be rejected. Yet with that one we ought to consider the fact that change is said to happen in the thing itself, not in God. Jeremiah says, "If they will repent of their way, I also will repent concerning all the evil that I have announced against them" [Jer. 18:8]. Thus, that change in man is followed by a change in the divine sentence, whether it pertains to the promise or

---

4. *ipso* Samuel 1564, Zurich 1580, Heidelberg 1603: *ipse* London 1576.

5. *hoc ipso loco* Samuel 1564, London 1576, Zurich 1580: *de Saule* Heidelberg 1603.

to the change. For as often as a sinner repents out of true faith, he is immediately freed from eternal destruction.

But the sentence about temporal punishments does not always change, even if the sinner repents very deeply. David repented of his adultery, yet the sentence of God that Nathan had pronounced stood fast [2 Sam. 12:13–14]. Moses repented, yet he was not able to enter into the land of promise [Num. 20:12]. So that statement holds true concerning eternal death, but not always concerning temporal punishments. Furthermore, this change proceeds not from the things themselves but from God. For Paul writes to Timothy as follows: "If perhaps God may grant them repentance" [2 Tim. 2:25]. And in the letter to the Philippians: "It is he who works in us both to will and to perform" [2:13]. We cannot even *think* well of ourselves as though of ourselves [2 Cor. 3:5]. And in the letter to the Corinthians, 15 [1 Cor. 15:10]: "I labored more than them all, yet not I but the grace of God that is in me."

They say: But it rests with us to give assent. On the contrary, even assent itself is from God. For we have a heart of stone; if it is not changed to become a heart of flesh, nothing is brought to pass [Ezek. 36:26]. And even if it seems a small thing for assent to be from us, as they claim, still once this much is ascribed to us we will have grounds for being able to boast. "For who has distinguished you?" Paul says. "What do you have that you did not receive? But if you received it, why do you boast as if you did not receive it?" [1 Cor. 4:7]. And: "It is not of the one who wills nor of the one who runs, but of God who has mercy" [Rom. 9:16]. Here Augustine says, "If something be left to us, Paul concludes nothing. For the proposition could be reversed, so as to read: 'It is not of God who has mercy, but of man who wills and runs.'"⁶ Paul says, "I know that good does not dwell in me, that is, in my flesh" [Rom. 7:18]. And Christ: "You did not choose me, but I chose you" [John 15:16]. David too says, "Incline my heart to your testimonies" [Psalm 119:36], and: "Create in me a clean heart, God" [Psalm 51:10]. But no one can create himself. We are said to be regenerated, but no one is regenerated by himself. Yet we are not regenerated like trunks or stones or sticks, for we have understanding, perception, and will. But it is God who causes us to understand, will, and perceive. Therefore, we must make a distinction among human beings, for some of them are regenerate, others are not. The one who is unregenerate can do nothing of himself. But after we have once been regenerated, we have our strength renewed and we are made cooperators with God.

3. At least in my judgment, we will understand more easily what it means for God to repent if we recall that he has one will which is secret, another which is revealed. For the secret will of God is firm and immutable. Therefore, the statement that God does not change should be referred to this will. God had decreed from the beginning that Saul would be king. This will is eternal and constant, and nothing happens without it. But he does not always reveal it fully and totally; he thinks it enough to manifest some part of it through the law or the prophets. This will can change—not because any change can be applicable to God, but because there is a change⁷ in something that

---

6. Augustine, *Enchiridion* 32 (*Enchiridion*, NPNF 1/3:248). Vermigli paraphrases somewhat.

7. *mutetur* Samuel 1564, London 1576, Zurich 1580: *mutatur* Heidelberg 1603.

people thought would last permanently. The will of God had been revealed: that there would always be a king in the line of Saul. For it was probable that this would happen. However, the other part of the will was secret and hidden. Hezekiah grows sick; Isaiah warns that he is going to die, for the nature of the disease was such that it seemed he was going to die [Isa. 38]. This will changed; the other, hidden will could not change.

But they object that our assertion that God's will is from eternity is a mere fiction, since nothing in God is either past or future. However, we are saying nothing that is foreign to the Scriptures. Paul says that God predestined us before the foundations of the world had been laid [Eph. 1:4]. If they do not believe us, let them consider the predictions. Jacob predicts that David will be king [Gen. 49:10]. How could this have happened if God's will does not extend into the future? But Paul says in the letter to the Romans, eleventh chapter [v. 29], "The gifts and the calling of God are without repentance." However, the sayings of Scripture should not be taken more widely than can be tolerated by the very passage in which they were written. For otherwise we will easily be drawn into error. In this passage Paul was discussing the covenant that God had made with the Jews, and he says that those allowances cannot be voided, and it is inevitable that many of the Jews will be converted to Christ at some point because the gifts and the calling of God are without repentance. Granted, others understand this passage to refer to those gifts which depend[8] on God's eternal predestination. For

---

8. *pendent* Samuel 1564, London 1576, Zurich 1580: *pendant* Heidelberg 1603.

predestination is certain and firm, they say, whereas the other gifts, either of present righteousness or of temporal things, can both be given and be taken away. For there are many who later fall away after having once believed. Theodoret says that the gifts are without repentance if one considers the nature of the things themselves, but if men fall away and are deprived of those things, this happens by their own vice.[9]

---

9. Cf. Theodoret of Cyrus, *Commentarius in omnes sancti Pauli epistolas* ad Rom. 11:29 (*PG* 82:181).
The heading "On temptation" introduces the next section. In between the present section and the next, Heidelberg 1603 inserts three paragraphs from Vermigli's Samuel commentary, on 1 Samuel 15, under the heading "In what sense Saul is told that his kingdom will be made firm forever, even though this benefit had already been marked out earlier for the tribe of Judah."

[CHAPTER 2: WHY AND HOW GOD TEMPTS MEN]

But before we get to the second heading, we need to discuss temptations. Etymologically the term derives from *nas*, which is "sign" or "token." For *nasa*, that is, "to tempt," obviously takes place when we want to understand something via a token or sign.[1] The Greeks use the term πειράζομαι, derived from πεῖρα, that is, experience. Let this be the definition: Temptation is probing intended to elicit knowledge of something not known. The formal cause is action. The end is knowledge,[2] knowledge of many things: of oneself, of one's weakness or virtue, of divine goodness or anger. But knowledge is not the ultimate end, because in upright men the end is often that they may conquer and get the crown, or, if they fall, that once relieved by divine help they may be humbled

---

1. The Latin verb *tento/tempto* (*tempt*) can also be translated *test*. The same is true of the Greek verb πειράζω, the term used in James 1:13, and its cognate πειρασμός (*temptation, test,* or *trial*).

2. Heidelberg 1603 inadvertently omits a line here by skipping from *Finis notitia* to *notitia non est*.

and be made more keen in the reverence and worship of God. The matter in which it exists is our mind, but it is occupied with all vices, which can be reduced to unbelief as their source. That the efficient cause of temptation is the flesh, the world, and the devil is not in question, but there is controversy about whether temptation can be ascribed to God.

5. James seems to deny this when he says that each one is tempted as a result of his own concupiscence and that God is not a tempter of evils [James 1:13]. And Paul seems to agree at least that not all temptations proceed from God, for he says that God makes a way of escape along with the temptation [1 Cor. 10:13]. But there are many temptations in which people are wretchedly caught and yet no way of escape is given them; instead they perish in those temptations. Besides this, we cannot grasp by reason how it happens that God punishes sins and yet by tempting becomes the author of them.

But these things notwithstanding, we must cling with all firmness to sacred Scripture, which occasionally ascribes temptation to God. In Deuteronomy [8:2] you have it written that God tested the sons of Israel in the wilderness so that he might know whether they would keep his precepts or not. Here you also have the end of the temptation. In the Psalm, David prays for God to test him [Psalm 26:2]. Job was tempted when God handed him over to Satan [Job 1:6–12]. In the first book of Samuel [16:14] you have it written that an evil spirit from the Lord entered Saul and troubled him. And in the second book of Samuel [24:1] David was incited by Satan to number the people. But in Chronicles 21 [1 Chr. 21:1] God is said to have incited David against Israel. Thus, the same action is attributed both to God and to Satan. Here we have a clear passage concerning Abraham [Gen. 22]. Ahab was enticed by the will of God, who sent a spirit to be a lying agent in the mouth of the prophets [1 Kings 22:22]. God hardened Pharaoh's heart [Ex. 9:12, etc.]. In Isaiah 6 [vv. 9–10] the prophet is sent to preach in order that seeing they may not hear, may be blinded, may be hardened, "lest," he says, "they be converted and I heal them." God sends them the word as a snare. And in Isaiah 63 [v. 17] the fathers complain, "Why have you led us astray and made our heart to wander from your ways?" Christ says to Philip, "Where will we buy bread?" He himself knew what he was about to do, yet he was speaking like this to test him [John 6:5–6]. And we implore God our Father, "Do not lead us into temptation" [Matt. 6:13].

There are some who wish to solve it like this: God tempts, that is, allows and permits others to tempt.[3] But this does not help at all. We should not shy away from the phrasing of the Scriptures. If Scripture says this, why should we not say it too? Moreover, this interpretation cannot apply to all the passages we have cited. For the Lord himself sends Isaiah, and God himself sends the lying spirit to Ahab, and Abraham was tempted by none other than God. Add to this that God's will is included in permission, and when the matter itself is settled, what help is it to change the terminology?

But come, let us consider the question: What evil is entailed if one attributes to God the act of tempting?

---

3. *tentare* Genesis 1569, London 1576, Zurich 1580: *tentari* Heidelberg 1603.

None at all. On the contrary, it is appropriate for him and befits his disposition, for he is eager to reveal both his justice and his mercy in all people. Those who are tempted belong either to the elect or to the damned: they are upright or wicked. If wicked, then just as their sins can be punished by other sins, as is explained in the letter to the Romans, first chapter [vv. 24–28], so they can be punished by temptations, in order that through these they may rush into various evils and, on account of these, be judged worthy of eternal punishments. If upright, then by tempting them God reveals and testifies how much value he sets on them. He is speedily present, he frees them, he crowns them, and he rewards them as victors with many excellent gifts. Or if they fall, that misfortune is temporary and ultimately has a happy outcome, as Paul explained [Rom. 5:3–4]: in this way their faith, hope, and charity are increased, while they see that they receive help and conquer their enemies by God's great favor, or because they are relieved from the burdens of their sins.

6. But for the present, let us respond to those arguments which seemed to persuade us otherwise. When James says that God does not tempt, he does not deny this altogether, but for the reason that those carnal Christians of his day were claiming that God tempted them, as though while they were sinning they should have been free from blame, just as the Libertines of our own day reportedly say. God, they claim, does all things in us, and therefore nothing is sin—not even thefts, murders, adulteries, etc. We certainly grant that God does all things, but the explanation for them is different insofar as they are done by us and insofar as they are done by God. Men

sin in committing those acts, since they are not drawn to them with the intention of cooperating with God, nor are they forced or compelled to them against their will. On the contrary, they are frustrated with themselves when they interpose obstacles to their own acts of sin. Therefore, let them consult their own conscience and then they will plainly see whether they sin against their will or in order to please God, or rather in order to satisfy their own unbridled lust. In just the same way, James is saying, "God does not tempt you in such a way that the cause and guilt of the things you do evilly and wickedly is to be transferred to him. You are tempted by your own concupiscence; that is, the reason you rush into your crimes is so that you may satisfy the lust urging you on." That is why the apostle used a simple negation to express what he meant there and wished to be denied in part. But as for Paul, when he says that God makes a way of escape along with the temptation, he is clearly speaking about those temptations which occasionally trouble the upright and elect. In such cases they generally have not only a way of escape but a reward.

We are less able to understand how it is not inconsistent with divine justice to punish sins yet also to impel men to sins by tempting. That is not surprising, for God can do more than we can understand. David once speaks about the understanding of these secret judgments in Psalm 73 [vv. 17–23]. He says that he was greatly troubled and that his distress was unbearable until he entered the sanctuary of God. Therefore, let us steadfastly believe that God does justly whatever he performs, and let us not remove from his providence or his power any of the things that take place. As for the way in which they harmonize with his justice or are not at odds[4] with it, if we do not understand this, let us believe with humility.

---

4. *non pugnent* Genesis 1569, London 1576: *pugnent* Zurich 1580, Heidelberg 1603.

[CHAPTER 3: WHETHER WE SHOULD PRAY TO BE SPARED TEMPTATION]

7. But let us continue: granted that they are from God, should we pray to avoid them or not? Let us make a distinction. Temptations are either adversities or suggestions to wicked crimes. If adversities, we ought not to pray that no adversities afflict us, since we have been plainly told by Paul, "Those who wish to live uprightly in Christ will suffer persecutions" [2 Tim. 3:12], and Christ holds out the cross to be borne by his people basically throughout their whole life [Luke 14:27]. But if we are worried that we may fail amid adversities or that God's glory may by hindered by them, we can pray for him to take them away. Paul prayed, and wished prayer to be offered by others, that he be freed from the persecutions that were threatening him in Judaea [Rom. 15:31]. Besides this, if while we are afflicted and our flesh is struggling, we piously ask the Father that it may please him to set us free, and if we yet prefer his will to our own, if this condition be fulfilled, we commit no sin. Christ taught this in the garden, when he prayed to his Father [Luke 22:39–42]. But if we consider the saints while by the grace of God they conduct them-

selves bravely amid those adversities, we will see that they rejoice in them because tribulation produces endurance, endurance produces proving [Rom. 5:3–4]. And Peter in the first chapter of his first letter says that the saints have joy in temptations [1 Pet. 1:6]. In fact, Paul boasts and gladly glories in his adversities because he considers them as proceeding not from the devil or from wicked men but from God's providence, and they are the instruments of his own reward and salvation [2 Cor. 11:23–30].

But if they are suggestions to evil, that is, to sins, then a distinction must be made, because in that case either there is a fall or there is victory. If victory is joined to them, this type is desirable to the saints, so that in these temptations they may subdue the devil, the flesh, and the world more and more each day. But if they are afraid of a fall, the fall itself is either temporary or permanent. If temporary, they should pray to avoid the temptation, as we do in the Lord's Prayer: "And do not lead us into temptation" [Matt. 6:13]. Christ taught this to his apostles when he said, "The spirit indeed is keen, but the flesh is weak. Watch and pray that you not enter into temptation" [Matt. 26:41]. And reason urges this, for we should pray to avoid all things that are opposed to God's will, and a fall against God's law is just such a thing. In fact, there is nothing that should displease us more than this, as is clear from the command, "You shall love your Lord with your whole heart and with your whole soul" [Matt. 22:37]. To this you may add: no one should be so confident in his own strength that he is not afraid in temptation. Therefore, we should always pray when in temptation. Yet we should not pray that no temptation may assail us, for God has decreed that our life be one of warfare. But upright and holy men do not fear for themselves on account of temptations that have a permanent and destructive outcome. For they know that God is their Father—something they could not believe if they suspected that he would abandon them. Moreover, they recognize that the calling and the gifts of God are without repentance, as is said in the letter to the Romans [11:29].

BIBLIOGRAPHY

Primary

Aquinas, Thomas, and Thomas Cajetan. *Aristotle, On Interpretation: Commentary by St. Thomas and Cajetan (Peri Hermeneias)*. Translated by Jean T. Oesterle. Milwaukee: Marquette University Press, 1962.

Aristotle. *On Interpretation*. Translated by Harold Cooke. In *Aristotle: The Categories, On Interpretation, Prior Analytics*. Cambridge, MA: Harvard University Press, 1973.

Pseudo-Aristotle. *On the Cosmos*. Translated by D. J. Furley. In *Aristotle: On Sophistical Refutations, On Coming-to-Be and Passing-Away, On the Cosmos*. Cambridge, MA: Harvard University Press, 1965.

Augustine. *Against Julian the Pelagian*. Translated by Matthew A. Schumacher. Washington, D.C.: The Catholic University of America Press, 1957.

———. *Against Two Letters of the Pelagians*. Translated by Robert Ernest Wallis. 1st ser., vol. 5 of *Nicene and Post-Nicene Fathers*, edited by Philip Schaff. Grand Rapids, MI: Eerdmans, 1978 reprint.

———. *The Catholic and Manichaean Ways of Life*. Translated by Donald A. Gallagher and Idella J. Gallagher. Washington, D.C.: The Catholic University of America Press, 2008.

———. *City of God*. Translated by Marcus Dods. 1st ser., vol. 2 of *Nicene and Post-Nicene Fathers*, edited by Philip Schaff. Grand Rapids, MI: Eerdmans, 1979 reprint.

———. *Confessions*. Translated by J. G. Pilkington. 1st ser., vol. 1 of *Nicene and Post-Nicene Fathers*, edited by Philip Schaff. Grand Rapids, MI: Eerdmans, 1979 reprint.

———. *The Enchiridion*. Translated by J. F. Shaw. 1st ser., vol. 3 of *Nicene and Post-Nicene Fathers*, edited by Philip Schaff. Grand Rapids, MI: Eerdmans, 1980 reprint.

———. *Expositions on the Book of Psalms*. Translated by A. Cleveland Coxe. 1st ser., vol. 8 of *Nicene and Post-Nicene Fathers*, edited by Philip Schaff. Grand Rapids, MI: Eerdmans, 1979 reprint.

———. *Eighty-Three Different Questions*. Translated by David L. Mosher. Washington, D.C.: The Catholic University of America Press, 2002.

———. *Of True Religion*. In *Augustine: Earlier Writings*, translated and edited by John H. S. Burleigh. Louisville: Westminster John Knox Press, 2006.

———. *On the Gift of Perseverance*. Translated by Robert Ernest Wallis. 1st ser., vol. 5 of *Nicene and Post-Nicene Fathers*, edited by Philip Schaff. Grand Rapids, MI: Eerdmans, 1978 reprint.

———. *On Grace and Free Choice*. In *Augustine: On the Free Choice of the Will, On Grace and Free Choice, and Other Writings*, edited and translated by Peter King. Cambridge: Cambridge University Press, 2010.

———. *On Rebuke and Grace*. Translated by Robert Ernest Wallis. 1st ser., vol. 5 of *Nicene and Post-Nicene Fathers*, edited by Philip Schaff. Grand Rapids, MI: Eerdmans, 1978 reprint.

———. *On the Trinity*. Translated by Arthur West Haddan, revised W. G. T. Shedd. 1st ser., vol. 3 of *Nicene and Post-Nicene Fathers*, edited by Philip Schaff. Grand Rapids, MI: Eerdmans, 1980 reprint.

———. *Letters 100–155*. In *The Works of Saint Augustine: A Translation for the 21st Century*, translated by Roland Teske. Hyde Park, NY: New City Press, 2003.

———. *The Literal Meaning of Genesis*. Vol. 1, bks 1–6. Translated by John Hammond Taylor. New York: Paulist Press, 1982.

Averroes [Ibn Rushd]. *Long Commentary on the* De Anima *of Aristotle*. Translated by Richard C. Taylor. New Haven: Yale University Press, 2009.

———. *Ibn Rushd's Metaphysics: A Translation with Introduction of Ibn Rushd's Commentary on Aristotle's Metaphysics, Book Lām.* Translated and edited by Charles Genequand. Leiden: Brill, 1984.

———. *Averroes' Tahafut Al-Tahafut (The Incoherence of the Incoherence).* Translated by Simon Van Den Bergh. 2 vols. in 1. London: E. J. W. Gibb Memorial Trust, 2012.

———. *Averroes' The Book of the Decisive Treatise Determining the Connection between the Law and Wisdom and Epistle Dedicatory.* Translated by Charles E. Butterworth. Provo: Brigham Young University Press, 2001.

Bernard of Clairvaux. *On Grace and Free Choice.* Translated by Daniel O'Donovan. Collegeville, MN: Liturgical Press, 1988.

———. *On Precept and Dispensation.* In *The Works of Bernard of Clairvaux*, vol. 1: *Treatises 1.* Translated by Conrad Greenia. Spencer, MA: Cistercian Publications, 1970.

Chrysostom, John. *Homilies on the Epistles of Paul to the Galatians and Ephesians.* Translated by Gross Alexander. 1st ser., vol. 13 of *Nicene and Post-Nicene Fathers*, edited by Philip Schaff. Grand Rapids, MI: Eerdmans, 1979 reprint.

Epiphanius. *The Panarion of Epiphanius of Salamis, Books II and III:* De Fide. Translated by Frank Williams. 2nd revised ed. Leiden: Brill, 2013.

Eusebius. *Preparation for the Gospel: Books 1–9.* Translated by Edwin H. Gifford. Eugene, OR: Wipf and Stock, 2002.

John of Damascus. *Saint John of Damascus: Writings.* Translated by Frederick H. Chase, Jr. Washington, D.C.: The Catholic University of America Press, 1981.

Junius, Franciscus. *De providentia Dei.* In *Francisci Iunii opuscula theologica selecta.* Edited by Abraham Kuyper. Amsterdam: Fred. Muller, 1882.

Lombard, Peter. *The Sentences.* Translated by Giulio Silano. 4 vols. Toronto: Pontifical Institute of Mediaeval Studies, 2007–2010.

Luther, Martin. *Luther's Works*, vol. 2: *Lectures on Genesis, Chapters 6–14.* Edited by Jaroslav Pelikan. Saint Louis, MO: Concordia Publishing House, 1960.

Melanchthon, Philip. *Loci communes rerum theologicarum, seu hypotyposes theologicae.* Mainz: Johann Schöffer, 1522.

———. *The Loci Communes of Philip Melanchthon.* Translated by Charles L. Hill. Boston: Meador, 1944.

Origen. *Commentary on the Epistle to the Romans, Books 6–10*. Translated by Thomas P. Scheck. Washington, D.C.: The Catholic University of America Press, 2002.

Prosper of Aquitaine. *The Call of All Nations*. Translated by P. De Letter. New York: Newman Press, 1952.

Rangueil, Claude. *Commentariorum in libros regum . . . Tomus 1*. Paris: Ex Office Nivelliana, 1621.

Zwingli, Ulrich. *Commentary on True and False Religion*. Edited by Samuel Macauley Jackson and Clarence N. Heller. 1929; reprint Durham, NC: Labyrinth, 1981.

———. "Reproduction from Memory of a Sermon on the Providence of God." In *On Providence and Other Essays: The Latin Works and Correspondence of Huldreich Zwingli*, edited by Samuel M. Jackson. Eugene, OR: Wipf and Stock, 1999.

Secondary

Anderson, Marvin. "Peter Martyr Vermigli: Protestant Humanist." In *Peter Martyr Vermigli and Italian Reform*, edited by Joseph C. McLelland, 65–84. Waterloo, ON: Wilfred Laurier University Press, 1980.
Aspray, Silvianne. *Metaphysics in the Reformation: The Case of Peter Martyr Vermigli*. Oxford: The British Academy, 2021.

Donnelly, John Patrick. *Calvinism and Scholasticism in Vermigli's Doctrine of Man and Grace.* Leiden: Brill, 1976.

Gibson, Margaret T. *Boethius, His Life, Thought, and Influence.* Oxford: Blackwell, 1981.

Huelin, Gordon. "Peter Martyr and the English Reformation." Ph.D. dissertation, University of London, 1954.

James, Frank A., III. "Confluence and Influence: Peter Martyr Vermigli and Thomas Aquinas on Predestination." In *Church and School in Early Modern Protestantism: Studies in Honor of Richard A. Muller on the Maturation of a Theological Tradition*, edited by Jordan Ballor, David Sytsma, and Jason Zuidema, 165–83. Leiden: Brill, 2013.

———, ed. and trans. *Predestination and Justification: Two Theological Loci.* Kirksville, MO: Truman State University Press, 2003.

Kirby, W. J. Torrance, Emidio Campi, and Frank A. James III, eds. *A Companion to Peter Martyr Vermigli.* Leiden: Brill, 2009.

McLelland, Joseph, ed. and trans. *Philosophical Works: On the Relation of Philosophy to Theology.* Kirksville, MO: Truman State University Press, 1996.

Muller, Richard A. *Dictionary of Latin and Greek Theological Terms*. Grand Rapids: Baker House, 1985.

———. *Post-Reformation Reformed Dogmatics: The Rise and Development of Reformed Orthodoxy, ca. 1520 to ca. 1725*, vol. 3: *The Divine Essence and Attributes*. Grand Rapids: Baker Academic, 2003.

Posti, Mikko. *Medieval Theories of Divine Providence 1250–1350*. Leiden: Brill, 2020.

Sharples, R. W. "Alexander of Aphrodisias on Divine Providence: Two Problems." *Classical Quarterly* 32, no. 1 (1982): 198–211.

Strype, John. *Memorials of the Most Reverend Father in God Thomas Cranmer . . .* London: George Routledge and Co., 1853.

INDEX

A

Abraham, 100, 142, 149, 163, 179
action(s), xiii, xxvi, 15, 29, 35, 61n3, 92–96, 177
   of devil(s), 56, 68, 69, 97, 122, 131, 179
      divine, vi, xiii, xiv, 9, 53, 56, 66, 70, 84, 85, 94,
         96, 97, 104, 107, 110–11, 131, 155,
         163, 170, 179
      evil, xviii, 48, 57, 68, 69, 70, 76, 79, 84, 86,
         91–92, 97, 101, 130, 134, 158
      human, viii, ix, xi, xv, xvi, xvii–xviii, xx, xxiii, 6,
         15, 28, 48, 49, 53, 57, 61, 67,
         69, 79, 85, 86, 88, 90, 91–98, 104, 105,
         106, 110, 111, 122–23, 137, 139, 141,
         143, 145, 150, 158, 165, 170
   of rational agents, viii, x, 94
   of spirits, 122
Adam, xxi–xxii, 88–89, 132, 158, 159n15
adultery, 180
Aeschylus, 131
affections, xvi, xviii, xx, 51, 52, 65, 67, 76, 100, 103,
   121, 145
Alexander of Aphrodisias, vi
Alexander of Hales, 147n2
Ambrose, 113–14, 145–46
Amos, N. Scott, xxvii–xxviii
Anderson, Marvin, xxvin35
angel(s), 5, 31, 69, 122, 124, 137, 138, 142, 156
anger of God. *See* wrath of God
Anselm, xxv, 57, 93

Apollo, 31
appetite, xviii, 8, 19n3, 103
Aratus, 66
Aristotle, Aristotelian, vi–vii, x–xi, xv, xxiv, xxv–xxvi, xxvin35, xxx, 11n1, 12n3, 15n7, 24, 30, 35n3, 37n5
Aspray, Silvianne, iv, xvii–xviii
astrologers, 30, 66n6
Athenians, viii, 31n11, 67
Augustine, vi, ix–x, xii, xiv, xv–xvi, xix, xxi, xxii, xxv, xxvin35, 2, 15, 26, 27–28, 34, 36, 42, 45, 53–54, 65, 71–72, 75, 83–86, 92–94, 97, 99–100, 101, 105, 106n2, 111–12, 113, 114–15, 119–20, 122–24, 126, 129, 133, 137–38, 145–46, 150, 152, 156–57, 164, 165, 170, 171, 172–73
Averroes, vii, xii, 8–9

B

baptism, 62
Barnes, Jonathan, 37n5
Bernard of Clairvaux, 100, 132, 138–39
blessedness, 88
Boethius, Anicius, ix, 35n3, 36–37
Bonaventure, 147n2
Bucer, Martin, xxvii, 146
Bullinger, Heinrich, i, 6n2, 165n4

C

Calvin, John, i, ii, xxvii, 6n2, 146
cause and effect, vi, x–xii, xvii, 13, 20, 36, 40–41, 47, 48, 52, 64, 76, 97–98, 121, 165

causes, natural, 5
chance, iii, v–vi, vii, ix–xi, xiv, 5, 11–12, 22
Chrysippus, 26
Chrysostom, John, 17–18, 39
Cicero, xxiv, 1, 3, 16, 26, 37n5
circumstances, xvi, 13n4, 40
command(s), xix, xx, 51, 53, 57, 81, 105, 107–8, 111–12, 121, 147, 184. *See also* will, God's, of sign/command
concupiscence, 47, 81, 178, 181. *See also* desire; lust
conscience, 49, 112, 162, 181
contingency, iii, v, vii, xi, xii–xiii, xxvi, 12–15, 26, 29, 31, 34–41
Cranmer, Thomas, i
curse(s), 45, 68, 71, 157
Cyprian, 119–20
Cyril, xxv, 39

D

damned (people), 6, 127, 132, 139, 180
David
    and census of Israel, 56, 130–31, 154, 178–79
    concubines defiled, 45
    cursed by Shimei, 45, 68, 71, 77, 82, 157
    predicted to be king, 174
    temporal punishments of, 68, 82, 172
    and temple, 164
death, xiii, 68, 76, 81, 91, 149, 161, 163, 172
deeds, xxi, 48–50, 71, 112, 114–15, 131, 150, 153, 154, 170

depravity, xvi, xviii, xxiii, 38, 67–70, 72, 77, 79, 80, 82, 83, 84, 93, 100, 103, 106, 120, 151–52, 155, 158, 161
desires, xxix, 117, 155–56. *See also* concupiscence; lust
devil(s), xviii, 28, 35, 47, 57, 59, 69–71, 76, 83, 88, 93, 97, 103, 105, 109, 110, 119, 120, 121, 122, 131, 139, 153–54, 157, 178, 179, 184
doctor, xxix, 28, 34, 55, 67–68
Donnelly, John Patrick, in1, xivn20, xviiin24, xixn25, xxivn32, xxvi, xxviin36, 35n3
Duns Scotus, John, 19n3

E

elect, election, 35, 73, 107, 108, 113, 144, 151, 180, 181. *See also* predestination
Empedocles, 26
enemies, xxix, 130, 153, 180
Engammare, Max, xxviiin39
Epicureans, 18–19
Epimetheus, 5
Epiphanius, 141
eternal life/death, 151, 172, 180
Euripides, 32n12
Eusebius, 26
evil, xiii, xv, xvi–xviii, xxiii, xxviii, 7, 8, 14, 42, 49, 50, 51, 54, 57, 59, 62, 65, 69, 79, 80–82, 84, 86–87, 88, 92, 93, 97, 101, 103, 105, 108–13, 117, 120, 121, 122, 123–24, 130–31, 134, 137, 139, 141–42, 144, 152, 153, 155, 156–58, 171, 178, 179–80, 181, 184
  cause of, iii, v, xv, xvii, 64–65, 70–72, 75–76, 103, 117, 121, 142

    as fault, 62
    as privation of goodness, xiv–xv, xvii, 60–61,
        63–64, 88
    problem of, xiii
    as punishment, 62
    purpose of, xxi–xxii, 14, 28, 71–72, 86–87, 124,
        130–31

F
faith, 6, 38, 172, 180
Fall, 88–89, 158
fate, v, vii–xii, xxiv, xxv, xxviii, 31, 37n5, 41–42
felix culpa (fortunate fault), 159
first man. *See* Adam
foreknowledge, of God, iii–iv, ix, xi, xxv, 1, 12, 16,
    33–34, 38, 39, 89, 123, 129–30
foresight. *See* foreknowledge of God
fortunate fault (*felix culpa*), 159
fortune, v, x–xi, 11–12, 30, 67
free will, ii, ix, xi, xxiv, xxv, xxvii, 12, 20n3, 101n5, 138,
    143. *See also* freedom
freedom, viii, ix, 12, 108, 138–39, 145. *See also* free will
Fulgentius, 106

G
Genequand, Charles, 8n5
gift, 6, 65, 88, 99, 174–75, 180, 185
glory, of God, 3, 10, 20, 23, 31, 42, 49, 87, 183
grace, 29, 38, 52, 73, 88, 101n5, 107–8, 110, 118, 134,
    139, 158, 172, 183
    withdrawn, xvi, xxiii, 52, 64–65, 100, 104, 108,
        117, 118, 121, 123, 125, 129, 131, 158

Gregory the Great, 150, 158–59
guilt, xvii, 56, 68, 91, 104, 108, 109, 181

H

habitus, xv, xxix, 61n3
heaven, heavenly land, 28, 31, 65, 81, 88, 115, 132, 138,
heavenly bodies, vii, 3, 18, 31n10
hell, 31, 59
Heraclitus, 26
Hesiod, xxiii, 25
Horace, xxiii, 100
Huelin, Gordon, in2
Hugh of St. Victor, 147n2

I

Ibn Rushd. *See* Averroes
idolatry, 51, 54–55
iniquity, 148. *See also* evil; sin
injustice, 48, 83, 132, 158

J

James, Frank A. III, xxivn33, 35n3, 165n4
Jerome, xxv, 22n7, 68–69, 117, 125–27, 133
Job, 28, 69, 70–71, 153, 178
John of Damascus, xx–xxi, xxv, 143–44
judgment, God's, xix, 6, 18, 48–49, 54, 68–69, 72, 77,
    82, 107, 108, 111–12, 114, 118, 121, 122, 125,
    127, 133, 147, 157, 180, 181
Julian (the Pelagian), 85, 156
Junius, Franciscus, 20n5
Justice, 60, 92, 109

of God, xix, xxii, 8, 14, 48, 67, 83, 91, 92, 106,
    117, 118, 122, 123, 128, 133, 134, 163,
    180, 181–82
Juvenal, xxiii, 67

knowledge, 3, 7, 9, 30, 35, 36, 39, 69, 75, 110, 143,
    162, 165, 177, 185
  God's, iv, viii, xxiii, 1, 6, 7–8, 9–10, 33, 36, 39,
    52, 56, 68, 71, 82, 83, 89, 110, 128,
    165, 178 *See also* foreknowledge, of God

L

law, xix, xx, 47, 48, 53, 62, 68, 73, 81, 89, 100, 105,
    107–8, 110, 111, 128, 131, 132–33,
    134, 147–48, 150–51, 162–63, 173, 184
  natural, xx, 163
liability, xix, xxxi, 91–92, 109
Libertines, 180
Lombard, Peter, 138, 147n2, 165
love, God's, 46
lust, xvii, xxiii, 68, 69, 89, 105, 110, 125, 151, 156, 158,
    181. *See also* concupiscence; desires
Luther, Martin, xxvii, 146, 170

M

magistrate(s), xxix, 67–68, 153
martyr(s), xxii, 28, 56, 128, 142
Masson, Robert, ii
McLelland, Joseph, iin4, xxix–xxx, xxxi, 6n2, 42n10,
    165n4
Melanchthon, Philip, ii, xxvii, 145
merit, 54, 133

Moses,
> and burning bush, 142–43
> intercession of, 162
> and Pharaoh, 51, 80
> temporal punishment of, 172

Muller, Richard A., xvn21, xxn26, 13n4, 61n3, 147n2

N

nature, viii, ix, xiii, xv, 16, 65, 92, 95, 101, 131, 149, 155
> corruption of, xvi, xviii, 8, 21, 79–80, 83, 88–89, 99
> of created things, xii–xiii, xvii, xxi, 2, 20, 21–23, 36–41, 61, 65, 70, 96–97, 107, 123, 127
> evil, 79–80, 83, 108
> God's, 14, 64, 107, 111, 121–22, 133
> good by, 79–80, 83, 88, 104, 108, 110, 125, 161
> human, xx, xxi, 73, 76, 132, 163–64. *See also*

nature, corruption of
> law of. *See* law, natural
> power of, 18, 20

Nebuchadnezzar, 28, 32, 40, 55, 81, 82, 130

necessity, xii–xiii, xxvi, 12–14, 26, 28–29, 34–42, 76, 138
> absolute, xxvi, 13, 34, 35n3
> conditional, 35n3
> of God, xxi, 153
> hypothetical, xxvi, 13, 34–35, 39–41
> simple. *See* necessity, absolute
> of sin. *See* sin, necessity of

Neoplatonism, vi, viii–ix, x, xxvin35

O

Oecolampadius, Johannes, xxvii, 146

Origen, xxv, 39
original sin. *See* sin, original
Ovid, xxiii, 32n12, 53

P

Pelagians, 85, 101n5, 156
penalty, 150
perfection, God's, ix, xxiii, 9n5, 19, 46, 100, 106, 152
Peripatetics, vi–vii, viii, xii, xxv, 22, 26
Phaethon, 31–32
philosophers, 26, 29–31, 35n3, 53, 64, 145
Plato, Platonists, viii, ix, xxiii, xxviii, 5, 7, 31n11, 130, 131n19, 142–43
Plotinus, viii
Posti, Mikko, iii–iv, vin9, viinl1, viii, xnn16–17, xin18, xxi–xxii, 9n5, 30n8
power of God, vii, x, xvi, 20, 25, 32, 57, 85, 86, 93, 144, 181
prayer, 51, 58, 65, 113, 119–20, 131, 161, 163, 178, 183–85
predestination, 6, 35n3, 42, 112, 130, 145, 151, 161, 174–75. *See also* elect, election
princes. *See* magistrates
privation, xv–xvii, xxvin35, xxix, xxxi, 60–62, 63, 65, 75, 88, 90, 91, 93–96, 104, 117, 158
Proclus, viii
Prometheus, 5
Prosper of Aquitaine, 101, 113–14
providence, i, ii–xxvii, , xxxii–xxxiii, 14–16, 17–20, 37, 38, 40–42, 62, 66–73, 77, 82, 84, 86–87, 104, 109, 118, 120, 122, 129, 155, 161, 164, 165n4, 184

all things subject to, 25–32, 41, 42, 69, 72–73,
    141–46, 181
benefits of faith in, 6
and chance. *See* chance
and contingency. *See* contingency
and creation, iv, 21, 25, 66
definition, iii–v, 1–3, 19–20
and effectual will. *See* will, God's, efficacious
and fate. *See* fate
grasped by natural reason, 3
immutable, iv, 35–36, 129, 161
and knowledge. *See* foreknowledge, of God;
knowledge, God's
    objections to, 5–10, 11–14, 27–28, 31–32
    and power, iv, 2–3, 20–22
    and secondary causes, v, xiii, 31–32
    and sin, xiii–xxiii. *See also* sin, cause of
    theories of, v–xiii, xxiii–xxiv, xxv–xxvi, 22
Pseudo-Aristotle, 37n5, 41n7
Pseudo-Fulgentius, 126n14
Ptolemy, Claudius, 30
punishment(s), xix, xxix, 19, 46, 48, 53, 54, 62, 64, 65,
    67, 70, 82, 91–92, 99–101, 109, 117,
    120, 122–23, 125, 130–31, 132, 144,
    148, 153, 154, 163, 178, 180, 181
    sin as, xxi, xxii, xxiii, 52, 60, 62, 91, 99–100,
        104, 130–31, 158, 180
    temporal, 172

R
Rangueil, Claude, 37n5
reason, xxiv, 3, 11, 15, 18, 19, 60, 106, 178, 184

regenerate, regeneration, 53, 87, 132, 138, 173
repentance, 50, 112, 115, 128, 149, 150, 171–72
    God's, i, xxxiv, 169–75
reprobate (people), 132, 133, 134, 144
    mind, 51, 84, 99, 117, 151, 155
reward, 180, 181, 184
righteousness
    original, 64n3
    ours, 89, 175

S

saints, 14, 56, 73, 76, 88, 112, 138, 144, 170, 183–84
salvation, 14, 47, 109, 113–14, 128, 133, 144, 149, 162, 184
Satan. *See* devil(s)
Saul, 31, 37–38, 40, 69, 162, 170–171, 173–74, 175n9, 178
Scaliger, Joseph Justus, i
scholastics, scholasticism, ii, iii, xiii, xv, xix, xxv–xvi, xxvii, xxx, 19n3, 20n4, 61n3, 94n8, 147
Semi-Pelagians, 114n9
Sennacherib, 28, 130
Sharples, R. W., vin10
simplicity, of God, vi, 19, 111, 144, 149
sin(s), 32, 45–50, 51–58, 59–62, 63–74, 75–77, 79–82, 83–98, 99–101, 103–4, 105–15, 117–34, 141–42, 144, 150, 151, 157–58, 162, 163, 178, 180–81, 183. *See also* evil; guilt; liability; privation
    actual, 132
    cause of, i, v, xiii–xxiii, xxv, xxxii, xxxiii, 45–50, 51–58, 59, 62, 63–74, 75–77, 79–82,

84, 87–89, 100, 103–4, 105–15, 117–34, 146, 152, 157–58
deformity of, 91–98
and degrees of human nature, 132
directed by God, 53, 86, 87, 89, 142
and free will, 132, 137–39
God as avenger, 46
God's hatred of, 46, 106
God's permission of, 83–90, 152–53
and God's will, 141–42, 144, 148, 154–55, 157–58
as motion, 53, 122–23
necessity of, xviii, 76, 89, 129, 132, 137
of omission, 94–96
original, xviii, 62, 73, 103, 132
as punishment. *See* punishment, sin as
punishment of. *See* punishment
as service to God, 67–73
spontaneous, 65–66
suggestions to, xviii, 76, 79–82, 83–84, 86, 87, 88, 103, 104, 108, 110, 121, 125, 183–84. *See also* temptation
temptation to. *See* temptation

Socrates, 31, 67
soul, 61n3, 66–67, 93, 127, 151
Stoics/Stoicism, vi, vii—viii, xii, xxiv, 16, 41
Strype, John, i–ii

T

temptation, 47, 119–20, 177–82, 183–85. *See also* sin, suggestions to

by God, i, xix, xxxiv, 47, 51, 110, 119–20, 178–82, 183
Theodoret of Cyrus, 175
Thomas Aquinas, iii, vi, x–xii, xvi, xix, xxi, xxii, xxv–xxvi, xxix, 11n1, 12n3, 19, 35n3, 61n4, 64n3, 94n8, 106n2
tyrants, 28, 48, 100, 128, 130, 142, 153

U
unbelief, unbelievers, 118, 178
unregenerate, 138, 173

V
Virgil, 18n2
vice(s), 81, 83, 93, 97, 108, 121, 125, 127, 137, 144, 157, 175
virtue, xix, 8n5, 28, 47, 80, 177
Vulgate, xxviii, xxxii, 22n7

W
will, 15, 52, 55, 56–57, 93–94,
    of devil, 70, 93, 122
    and fault, 52
    God's, iv, v, x, xii, xiv, xvii, xix–xxi, xxiii, xxvi, 1, 3, 5, 6, 16, 19, 21, 25, 28, 33, 36, 37–39, 42, 47, 48–50, 52, 53, 54–58, 62, 64, 67, 68–72, 75, 82, 84–89, 91, 97–98, 100–101, 104, 107, 108–9, 111–15, 118, 121–24, 126, 128–31, 133, 134, 137, 141, 144–45, 147–154, 158, 161–65, 173–74, 179, 183, 184

efficacious, iv, xix–xxi, xxvi, 16, 84, 86–87, 147–51
of good pleasure, 124, 144, 147–51, 162
permissive, xx–xxi, 84–89, 104, 122, 137, 151–53, 179
revealed, xx, 149, 173
secret, xx, 149, 173
of sign/command, xix–xx, xxvi, 31, 107, 108–9, 111–12, 147–51
unity of, xix–xx, xxv, 33, 49, 111, 161
human, viii, ix, xvi, xvii–xviii, xx, 13, 26, 30, 37–38, 40, 52, 53–55, 57, 61, 64, 67, 68, 69, 71–72, 73, 75, 76, 80, 83–84, 87–89, 93–98, 103, 105, 107, 108, 110, 111, 119–24, 130, 131, 133, 138–39, 141, 154, 157, 161–65, 172–73, 181, 183. *See also* free will
word of God, xv, 15, 19, 25, 61, 76, 95, 109, 114, 118–19, 130, 154, 179
work(s), 17, 18, 26–27, 46, 66, 70, 71, 94, 95, 96–97, 165. *See also* deeds
of evil men, xvii, 70–72, 153
of God, xvii, 3, 14, 25, 26, 27, 50, 54, 59, 66, 67, 70–72, 73, 82, 84, 86, 112, 139, 143, 163, 165, 172
good, 6, 47, 49
wrath of God, 48, 85, 87, 156

Z
Zeus, 37n5
Zwingli, Ulrich, xxvii, 6n2, 84, 127–28, 133, 146

Made in the USA
Monee, IL
15 September 2024

65830851R00144